LONDON BEFORE THE CONQUEST

BY

W. R. LETHABY

British Library Cataloguing-in-Publication Data
A catalogue record for this book is available from the
British Library

Contents

A Short Introduction to the History of London

London has been a major settlement since being founded by the Romans, who named it Londinium, two thousand years ago. As the capital city of England, it is also the country's most populous city, with its metropolitan area housing over thirteen million inhabitants and taking the crown of the most visited city in the world. At the centre of this, now gargantuan metropolis, is an area known as the City of London, covering only 2.9Km 2 – still contained within its medieval boundaries. Due to this peculiar quirk of history, 'the City of London' actually qualifies as the smallest city in England.

The first sizable conurbation appeared in the region in 43 AD, but only lasted seventeen years until it was ransacked and burned by the Iceni tribe led by Queen Boudica. Its next incarnation was more successful when in the second century AD it acted as the capital of the Roman province of Britannia – its population then swelled to sixty thousand. This settlement survived until the fifth century when it was largely abandoned due to the collapse of the Roman Empire. It was then the turn of the Anglo-Saxons to become the dominant force in the area, building it up into a major trade port by the mid seventh century. This success became very difficult to maintain as the following centuries found London's inhabitants having to defend themselves against an onslaught of Viking invasions and their subsequent occupation of much of the east and northern parts of England.

The City continued to grow throughout the Middle Ages, for the most part after the Battle of Hastings in 1066 AD and the conquest of the Normans. William, Duke of Normandy, was crowned in the newly finished Westminster Abbey and consolidated his presence by ordering the construction of the Tower of London and Westminster Hall. Over the next hundred years the central government of England became fixed in the area of the City of Westminster while the City of London, its neighbour, flourished into England's most populous city (as well as its commercial centre). This district grew and grew until the disastrous onset of the Black Death in the mid fourteenth century.

The Black Death resulted in a third of the City of London's inhabitants being lost to the pandemic. It was estimated to have killed over one hundred million people throughout Europe. This however, was not to be London's only catastrophe. The Great Plague of 1665 which killed 100,000 people was immediately followed by the Great Fire of London in 1666. This particularly devastating blaze swept through the central parts of the city, destroying many of the predominantly wooden buildings, all in all resulting in the loss of 13,200 houses, 87 parish churches, St. Paul's Cathedral and most of the city authority's buildings. The destruction was on a large scale, but London was not to be broken. Under the supervision of the surveyor Robert Hooke, a rebuilding programme was ordered and the city underwent a ten year period of reconstruction.

In the wake of this rebuilding some of the city's most iconic buildings and areas appeared, such as St Paul's Cathedral and the district of Mayfair. This bustling capital city became a hub for both business and culture, and the place to be for forward thinking academics. The famed scholar Samuel Johnson (1709-1784) once commented:

'You find no man, at all intellectual, who is willing to leave London. No, Sir, when a man is tired of London, he is tired of life; for there is in London all that life can afford.'

During the Victorian era London became the world's largest city as it gradually expanded to join up with the surrounding counties who operated under the banner of the London County Council. It was seen as a city of progress, and thousands flocked to be a part of the industrial and economic development. This sudden enlargement led to paralysing traffic congestion however, which required a novel solution. This resulted in the construction of the world's first underground rail network, a shining example of the engineering prowess of a nation on the up. Despite such success stories, the twentieth century brought with it a new adversary to deal with, the air raid. Although significant bombardments were made in the First World War, it was the Second World War that saw the catastrophic potential of this new aerial technology. The German Luftwaffe killed over thirty thousand inhabitants and reduced large tracts of the city to rubble. Before the war London reached its peak population at around 8.6 million in 1939, but following the conflict its numbers fell to an estimated 6.8 million in the 1980s.

London continues to be a hugely influential, cosmopolitan capital, and remains a hive of cultural innovation. It has a long and multi-faceted history and it is hoped that this brief introduction has inspired the reader to find out more.

London and the Thames, from Speed's Map, 1610

LONDON BEFORE

THE CONQUEST

BY

W. R. LETHABY

"Now would I fain
In wordys playn,
Some honoure sayen,
And bring to mynde
Of that auncient cytie
That so goodly is to se."
—Fabyan.

"Lundres est mult riche cite,
Meliur n'ad en Cristienté
Pur vaillance, ni melx assisé,
Melx gaurnie, de grant prisee;
Al pe del mur li curt Tamise
Pur li vent la marchandise
Des tutes les qui sunt
U marcheans Crestiens vient."
Roman de Tristan.

INTRODUCTION

A great burh, Lundunaborg, which is the greatest and most famous of all burhs in the northern lands.—*Ragnar Lodbrok Saga.*

Of the hundreds of books concerning London, there is not one which treats of its ancient topography as a whole. There are, it is true, a great number of studies dealing in an accurate way with details, and most of the general histories incidentally touch on questions of reconstruction. Of these, the former are, of course, the more valuable from the topographical point of view, yet even an exhaustive series of such would necessarily be inadequate for representing to us the ancient city in a comprehensive way.

In an inquiry as to the ancient state of a city, a general survey, besides bringing isolated details into due relation, may suggest new matter for consideration in regard to them, and offer fresh points of proof. For instance, the extra-mural roads were directed to the several gates, the gates governed the internal streets, while these streets ran through wards, and gave access to churches and other buildings.

The subject of London topography is such an enormous one, and the involutions of unfounded conjecture are so manifold, that an approximation to the facts can only be obtained by a critical resifting of the vast extant stores of

9

evidence. In the present small essay I have, of course, not been able to do this in any exhaustive way; but I have for years been interested in the decipherment of the great palimpsest of London, and, in trying to realise for myself what the city was like a thousand years ago, I have in some part reconsidered the evidences. The conclusions thus reached cannot, I think, be without some general interest, although from the very nature of my plan they are presented in the form of notes on particular points, and discussions of opinions commonly held, with little attempt at unity, and none at a pictorial treatment of the subject.

Of mistaken views still largely or nearly universally accepted which will be traversed here, I may mention a few salient examples. For instance, Stow's opinion that London Bridge before the twelfth century was far to the east of the later bridge, and that the mural ditch was a mediæval work; Stukeley's opinion that the old approach through Southwark pointed on Dowgate, that Old Street was the great west-to-east Roman road, and that Watling Street in the city carries on the name of a street which formerly lay across its course, running from London Bridge to Newgate. From more recent writers, I may cite Mr. J. E. Price's idea that the Cheap was not at an early time a thoroughfare; Mr. J. R. Green's views,[1] as given in his *Conquest of England*, that Saxon London "grew up on ground from which the Roman city had practically disappeared"; that the Roman north gate

and the north-to-south street were considerably to the east
of the line of Bishopsgate and Gracechurch Street; and that
the Tower of London was built by the Conqueror on "open
ground only recently won from the foreshore of the river."
The plan which accompanies these views is equally visionary;
a large quarter of the city east of St. Paul's is lettered "The
Cheap"; there is no Aldgate Street (now Leadenhall Street),
the Langbourne appears as a stream, and there is a curious
selection of churches, amongst which is St. Denis, for which
we are referred to a note in Thorpe's *Ancient Laws*, regarding
a gift of London property to the monastery of *St. Denis in
Francia*. Mr. Loftie holds that Aldgate was first opened in
the time of Henry I., and that no mediæval gate exactly
occupied a Roman site; that the eastern road turned off
outside Bishopsgate; that Ludgate was still more recent than
Aldgate, and that it only opened on the Fleet river; that the
Strand was not a route before mediæval days; that there was
a Roman citadel on the high ground from the Walbrook
to Mincing Lane, and that the Langbourne was a ditch
to this stronghold. In the last book on the subject, called
Mediæval London, we are again told of the oblique Roman
Watling Street; Cheap is described as "a great square"; and
it is assumed that not only the Langbourne, but the equally
mythical Oldbourne, supplied the city with water.

11

*Fig. 1.—Goddess of Hope
(Roman Bronze found in London).*

I have here only rapidly set down a few of the opinions which are still current[2]—views which are repeated, embellished, and amplified to distraction in more popular writings, and set out with much appearance of exactitude in most misleading maps.

The whole question, indeed, of the early topography of London is overloaded on a quite insufficient basis of fact, and quakes and gives way under the least pressure of examination.

CHAPTER I

ORIGINS—THE LEGEND OF LONDON—
THE BRITISH CHURCH—
THE ENGLISH COME TO LONDON—
ALFRED'S LONDON

Like as the Mother of the gods, they say,
Old Cybele, aray'd with pompous pride,
Wearing a diademe embattild wide
With hundred turrets, like a turribant:
With such an one was Thamis beautifide;
That was to weet the famous *Troynovant*.
The Faerie Queen.

Origins.—The earliest historic monument of London is its name. The name Londinium first appears in Tacitus under the date of A.D. 61 as that of an *oppidum* "not dignified with the name of a colony, but celebrated for the gathering of dealers and commodities."

Dr. Guest propounded the theory that the city was founded by Plautius, the general of Claudius: "When in 43 he drew the lines round his camp, he founded the present metropolis.... The name of London refers directly to the marshes."[3] Dr. Guest is here apparently in agreement with

15

Godfrey Fausett's view that the name London represents Llyn-din, the Lake-fort.[4] Many attempts have been made to explain the name, by Camden and others, from other Welsh roots, but nothing is more uncertain than the origin of place-names.[5]

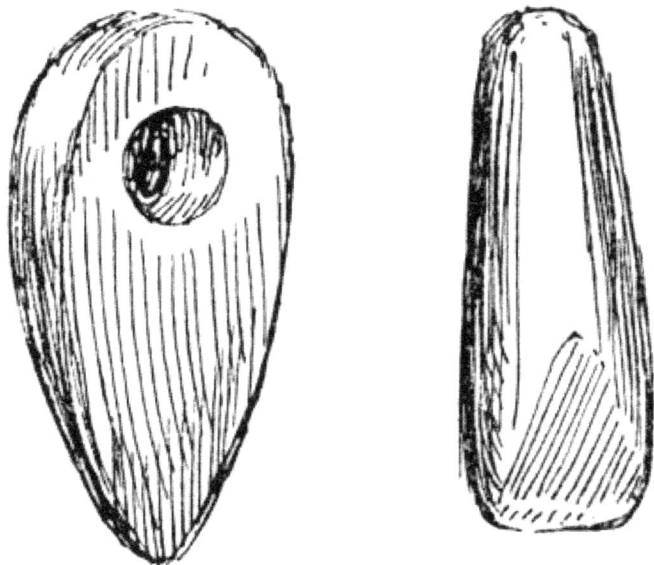

Fig. 2.—Stone Weapons from the Thames.

The tradition given by Geoffrey of Monmouth was that London was called Caer-Lud after a King Lud. Recent writers compare this name with Lydney, on the Severn, where a temple has been found dedicated to Nodens (or Lud), and say that London means Lud's-town,[6] thus coming round to Geoffrey.[7] This Nodens, who was worshipped at Lydney "as god of the sea," appears "in Welsh as Nudd and Lludd, better known in English as Lud."[8] Another Celtic deity, Lug or Lleu, is said to have left his name in a similar way to Lyons, Leyden, and Laon, "each originally a Lugdunum or Lugo's Fort."[9]

Fig. 3.—Centre of Celtic Bronze Shield from the Thames.

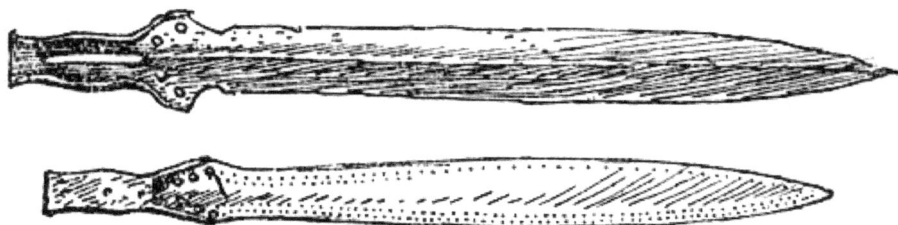

Fig. 4.—Celtic Bronze Swords.

All these derivations seem mere conjectures, but the last from Lud is at least in harmony with tradition. Yet that very tradition may be founded on an attempt to provide an origin for the name, according to the principles which derived Gloucester from Claudius and Leicester from the Welsh Lyr.[10]

Fig. 5.—Coin of Cunobelin (enlarged).

It is difficult to see why under Dr. Guest's theory of Roman foundation, which is accepted in Green's *Making of England*, London should have had a Celtic name at all. Dr. Rhys says that the name was so ancient that the Roman attempt to change it to Augusta failed. That it was a local habitation before the Roman occupation seems to be almost proved by the prehistoric and early objects found on the site, amongst which are four or five inscribed coins of Cunobelin (Cymbeline) found in the city and neighbourhood; and it seems unlikely that a mere camp in 43 would have grown in 61 to the important place celebrated by Tacitus. Green says that the chief argument against its antiquity is the fact that the great Watling Street[11] passed wide of the city through Westminster, but surely there might be settlements below the lowest convenient passage of the river. The Watling Street, if earlier than the settlement, *did not in any case* cause the town to be built on its course, and, if later, it *did not* pass through the settlement. The argument, indeed, goes only to prove that either the Watling Street or London could not be where they are. Or, at most, it might be contended that the road was more likely to go to the town than the town was to settle on the road, and as they are not together, that the road may be earlier than the town; but of actual time the argument can show nothing. Altogether, nothing can be got out of this argument, and we are free to conclude that London is at least as old as our era.

Fig. 6.—Bronze Lamp, Roman, found in London.

The Legend of London.—Geoffrey of Monmouth's history of the Britons, written about 1130, contains a legend of the founding of London, which tells how Brutus, migrating from Troy to this western island, formed the design of building a city. On coming to the Thames he found on its bank a site most suitable for his purpose, and building the city there, he called it New Troy—*Troiam Novam*, "a name afterwards corrupted into Trinovantum." Here King Belinus afterwards built a prodigious tower and a haven for ships under it, which the citizens call after his name—Billingsgate—to this day. Still later King Lud surrounded the city with strong walls and towers, and called it Caer Lud; when he died his body was buried by the gate which is called in the British tongue Porthlud, and in the Saxon Ludesgata.

All this was received as firm history, until, with the critical reaction against "mere legend," it was all cast aside as fiction and forgery. From this extreme position there is again a reaction, and Geoffrey is allowed to have founded on earlier writings, now in part lost, and to have embodied genuine folk-stories and lays of British origin.[12]

The Britons like all peoples must have had a legend of their origin, and this one falls in too well with the general type of such legends for it to be anything else than true folk-lore. Indeed, the legend of the derivation from Brutus, and of his Trojan antecedents, appears centuries before Geoffrey in Nennius, and the steps of its evolution can be easily retraced. The Britons required an eponymous founder for their race as much as the Israelites required an Israel, or the

Romans a Romulus. This founder (a supposititious Brittus) was at some time equated with Brutus, and Britain, like so many cities in Italy, was said to be founded by a fugitive from Troy. From Cæsar we learn that a tribe of the Trinobantes was found by him near the north bank of the Thames. This true name of a tribe was in the legend made to yield a city, Trinovantum, and this step had been made before Bede and Nennius, who say that Julius defeated the Britons near a place called Trinovantum. This name in turn was explained by Geoffrey as being "a corruption" of Troy-novant. Thus "New Troy" again quite naturally connects "Brutus" (or Brittus) with "Old Troy," and the whole scheme may date back to Romano-British days.

This is the natural genesis of the myth of the founding of London, and it is evident on the face of it that it is not the clever work of a romance-writer embroidering on Nennius, but genuine folk-lore or imperfect science.

In the twelfth century the story was accepted as gospel in London. The (so-called) Laws of the Confessor provide that the Hustings Court should sit every Monday, for London was founded after the pattern of Great Troy, "and to the present day contains within itself the laws and ordinances, dignities, liberties, and royal customs of ancient Great Troy."[13] FitzStephen refers back to the same origins, and the same were adduced in a dispute with the Abbot of Bury as to market privileges which the Londoners claimed dated from the foundation of the city before Rome was founded. [14] Perhaps there is no absolutely certain proof that the Troy story was told in London before Geoffrey's time, but it seems likely, judging from the number of detailed London allusions in Geoffrey's work, that there was a British and Arthurian tradition current there before he wrote. Of the latter, at least, one positive scrap of confirmation may be offered. Amongst the names appended to a deed at St. Paul's dated 1103 is that of Arturus, a canon. This carries back the use of the name Arthur to the time of the Conquest, and we may be certain that where the name was in use, there the story of the "noble King of the Britons" was told.[15] There was a strong contingent of the Celts of Brittany in the Conqueror's army, and to them the invasion must have seemed a re-conquest of Britain, and stories of the time before the Saxons took the "crown of London" must have been revived and spread abroad.

There is some slight possibility that when Geoffrey tells us that Belinus made a wonderful structure at the quay called after him Billingsgate, he was not merely playing on the name of "some Saxon Billings," as has been said, for Belinus is recognised as the best known of the Celtic gods, and the name has been found in many inscriptions. [16] Geoffrey again tells us that Belinus constructed the great Roman roads in Britain, and we cannot be asked to suppose that the Roman roads were said to be the work of

Belinus because the same Saxon Mr. Billings kept a posting-house.[17] The weight of evidence seems to allow of the view that there really were some remarkable Roman structures at the Tower and Billingsgate which tradition pointed to as the work of the Celtic culture-god Belinus, or of a king who bore his name. Some remnants of a building seem to have had the myth attached to them in the Middle Ages. Harrison, giving a version of the story, says of the Tower, "In times past I find this Belliny held his abode there, and thereunto extended the site of his palace in such wise that it extended over the Broken Wharf and came farther into the city, in so much that it approached near to Billingsgate, and as it is thought, some of the ruins of his house are yet extant, howbeit patched up and made warehouses, in that tract of ground in our times" (Holinshed). Belinus seems at times to have been confused with Cæsar, and so we get the Cæsar's Tower of Shakespeare and other writers. Stow, writing of the same "ruins," says, "The common people affirm Julius Cæsar to be the builder thereof, as also of the Tower itself."

Nennius uses the name Belinus for Cassibelaunus, which latter, indeed, is evidently derived from the former; for he speaks of Belinus (Cassibelaunus) fighting against Cæsar. A parallel passage in Geoffrey gives Belinus the command of the army of Cassibelaunus, but in the account of the battle which follows we have no word of Belinus, but "Nennius," a brother of Cassibelaunus and Lud, takes his place and perishes from a blow of Cæsar's sword, *Crocea Mors*. "Nennius" was then buried at the North Gate of "Trinovantum" with the sword that had slain him.[18] All this is too confused to work out in detail, but it almost looks like a repeated echo of some legend which made Cassibelaunus fall in a *personal* encounter with Cæsar. At bottom perhaps it may have been some inscription, or coin, lettered Cuno-belin, which associated the name of Belinus with a gate of London. Such coins have been found in London. We can only be certain that at the beginning of the twelfth century the existing name of the gate was explained by a Celtic word.

Fig. 7.—Coin of Claudius and another of Constantius, the latter inscribed London (p.lon.). enlarged.

As to Geoffrey's other story, which put a brazen man on a brazen horse over Ludgate, it would appear to be a variation on the story of the brazen horse of Vergilius, but I think we may find the origin of its localisation at Ludgate in the well-known coin of Claudius, which shows an equestrian image above an arch of triumph lettered DE BRITANN. This coin is one of those occasionally found in England, and we may suppose ancient antiquaries reasoned thus about it: "It must represent a city gate in Britain; the most important is the gate of London—Ludgate." Why was the brazen horse put there? "For a terror to the Saxons" (so in Geoffrey). Who put it there? "King Lud himself, or Cadwaladr, the last British king." When did it disappear? "When the Saxons entered the city"—as in the Prophecy of Merlin, "The brazen man upon a brazen horse shall for long guard the gates of London.... After that shall the German Worm (dragon) be crowned and the Brazen Prince be buried." It was supposed to have been the palladium of Caer Lud, "and the sygte ther of the Saxons aferde."[19]

For me the old British Solar God lights up the squalor of Billingsgate. The Sea God, Lud, and the brazen horse give me more pleasure than the railway bridge at Ludgate. Cæsar's sword at Bishopsgate and the head of Bran buried on Tower Hill are real city assets. London is rich in romantic lore. In her cathedral Arthur was crowned and drew the sword from the stone. Here Iseult attended the council called by King Mark. From the quay Ursula and her virgins embarked; Launcelot swam his horse over the river at Westminster, and from it Guinevere went a-maying. Possibly some day we may be as wise as Henry the Third, and put up statues to Lud and his sons at the gate which bears his name for a memorial of these things.

The British legend of the foundation of London has left one tangible legacy to us even to this day in the Guildhall giants, Gog and Magog, who represent the Gogmagog of Geoffrey, a giant of the primitive people overcome by the Britons—the Magog of the Bible, who stands for the Scythian race. Thus the Guildhall Magog really represents the Ivernian race in Britain.

So much for the legend. My final opinion is that the story of Caer Lud arose in an attempt to bring together the names of London, Ludgate, and Lludd, a Welsh god, and this may have been Geoffrey's work. I cannot find that the form Caer Lud was used in Welsh documents of an earlier date, although in a recent history of Wales London is so called throughout. If a single instance of "Caer Lud" could be adduced it would be different, but till that is done all derivations from Ludd must go by the board. The association of Belinus with London may in a similar way have been brought about by false etymology.[20]

The British Church in London.—It is not proposed to deal with the age of Roman occupation here, but we may devote a few lines to the British Church as a link between Roman and Saxon days. Before the imperial forces were withdrawn from Britain the dwellers in the cities would have been completely Romanised in manners and speech, and must have shared in some degree in the general change of aspect towards Christianity.

Fig. 8.—Christian Monogram from Cakes of Pewter found at Battersea.

The subject of British Christianity has lately been re-examined by Mr. Haverfield[21] and by Dr. Zimmer, the great Celtic scholar. The legend given by Bede as to the introduction of Christianity by a King Lucius is thought to have arisen in Rome about the beginning of the seventh century. It is, however, held that there must have been a gradual infiltration of the Gospel during the third century at latest, and that in the next century there was in Britain a fully organised Church in contact with, and a lively member of, the Church in Gaul. At the beginning of the fifth century there was an overwhelming majority of Christians, and Dr. Zimmer shows good reasons for thinking that Ireland had already been evangelised by the first great wave of monasticism before St. Patrick went there as its first bishop in 432. Patrick himself was born in 386, some 70 or 80 miles from London along the Watling Street, at Bannaventa. His family had been Christians for generations; his great-grandfather was a presbyter.

The story of St. Alban, the existence of whom there is little reason for doubting, carries us back to the end of the third century. Dr. Zimmer considers that the edict of Leo the Great (454) as to celebrating Easter reached the Church in Britain and Ireland before it was cut off from dependence on the Roman see. Latin must have continued in use in the Church in such places as Exeter and Bodmin, and in Wales, Strathclyde, and Ireland, from the time when it was current as a Romano-British speech.

According to Geoffrey there were three archbishoprics in Britain: London, York, and the city of Legions (Caerleon), representing South and North Britain and Cambria respectively. In the year 314 the names of three British bishops are given as being present at the Council of Arles: Eborius of York, Restitutus of London, and Adelfius, "de civitate colonia Londinensium." Haddan and Stubbs accept the record; so also do Haverfield and Zimmer, who substitute Lincoln for the last. Many British bishops were also at the Council of 359. Guitelin, a bishop of London in the fifth century, is mentioned by Nennius.

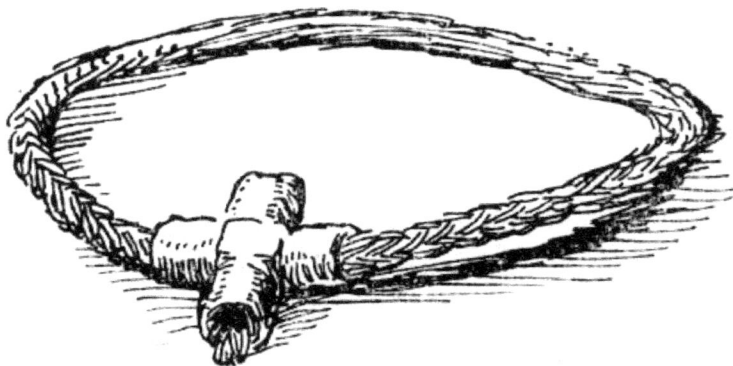

Fig. 9.—Bronze Bracelet.

According to Geoffrey, again, the Archbishops Theon of London and Thadiock of York fled from their charges about 586. Now a small scrap of evidence has been recently brought to light as to the existence of these bishops by Mr. Round, who shows that a church dedicated to a St. Thadiock remained at Monmouth in the twelfth century. Again, Jocelyn of Furness (cited by Stow), a writer of the twelfth century, gives a list of the British Bishops of London, which Bishop Stubbs is inclined to accept.[22] From Bede, moreover, we gather that Pope Gregory at first intended to establish the southern archbishopric, not at Canterbury, but at London. Then finally we have the curious claim made by St. Peter's, Cornhill, to be the first church in the kingdom. This legend appears in Jocelyn of Furness. Bishop Foliot at

the same time made the former dignity or London the basis
of a claim against Canterbury.

Fig. 10.—Head of a Pin.

It is often assumed that British London fell violently,
and that the old institutions were obliterated, but a
comparison of evidence gathered from the British legends
with the Saxon Chronicle suggests that it is just possible that
the English may have entered the city on terms, as at Exeter,
where Briton and Saxon long dwelt side by side.

Of the time after the English invasion Bishop Stubbs writes: "There were still Roman roads leading to the walls and towers of empty cities; camps, villas, churches were become, before the days of Bede, mere haunted ruins. It is not to be supposed that this desolation was uniform; in some of the cities there were probably elements of continuous life: London, the mart of the merchants; York, the capital of the North; and some others, have a continuous political existence, although they wisely do not claim an unbroken succession from the Roman municipality." Freeman held a similar view: "London is one of the ties ... with Celtic and Roman Britain." Mr. Coote believed that Roman institutions survived all changes, and Thomas Wright says: "We have no reason for believing that this city, which was a powerful commercial port, was taken and ravaged by the Saxon invaders; a rich trading town, it appears to have experienced no check to its prosperity."

Fig. 11.—Enamelled Plate.

On the question of a Roman Church in Britain, however, Thomas Wright took up a position of extreme scepticism, stating that there were no remains, that historical references were forgeries, or flourishes of rhetoric, that Gildas was a pretence, and that it was impossible to say how Christianity reached Cornwall and Wales. The more recent position would be the opposite of all this, and considerable material evidence can be produced, which has been crowned within the last few years by the discovery of the foundations of a

Roman church at Silchester, which may be the cathedral of the city, for there Geoffrey says Manganius was bishop in 519. The later Irish, Cornish, and Welsh Churches are only parts of the common British Christianity, which ultimately got shut up into the corners of the land by the English invasion, but originally formed part of the one Church which was an offshoot from the Church of Gaul, the original centre of which was at Lyons. As Lyons derived from Rome, and London from Lyons, so the Church in the western and northern provinces of England derived from London, and the western provinces in turn handed on the faith to Ireland. Even the Celtic rule as to Easter was the Roman use up to the middle of the fifth century.

Fig. 12.—Cross from Mosaic Pavement found in London.

The monumental evidences, certain or doubtful, for the British Church found in London are:—

(1) Eight small cakes of pewter found at Battersea, and stamped with the ×Ñ monogram. They are now in the British Museum. There are two varieties of stamps; one has the letters Á.Ù. added to the monogram; in the other the words SPES IN DEO surround it. These most interesting inscriptions are supposed to be of the fourth century (Fig. 8).

(2) A chain bracelet of bronze with a simple cross attached, now in the British Museum (Fig. 9).

(3) A disc forming the head of a pin, on it an imperial head and a cross; probably Constantine's vision, as suggested by Roach Smith (Fig. 10).

(4) An enamelled plate on which two beasts appear drinking from a vase, as so often found in early Christian art; probably, as suggested by Roach Smith, of the fifth or sixth century (Fig. 11).

(5) An ornamental cross on a mosaic pavement (Fig. 12). The last three have been figured by Roach Smith, and are also in the British Museum.

(6) A lead funeral cist found in Warwick Square with the ☧ X monogram, or possibly only a star form, now in the British Museum.

There is every probability that St. Germain of Auxerre, on his way to St. Albans, preached to the British citizens of London against the heresy of their countryman Pelagius about 429.

Fig. 13.—Saxon Spear.

The English come to London.—It is generally held that London was walled towards the end of the fourth century. Mr. Green suggests, indeed, that it and the fortresses of the Saxon shore mentioned in the *Notitia* were fortified as a provision against the attacks of Picts and Saxons. The need for such protection was soon made evident, for the only event chronicled in regard to London during the early period of the English Conquest is that in 457, after the battle of "Creganford," the Britons fled from Kent to London. Then comes silence for a century and a half, until 604, when it is told how Mellitus, a companion of St. Augustine, was sent to preach to the East Saxons, whose king, Sebert, a nephew of Ethelbert, gave Mellitus a bishop's stool in London. Although there is no definite statement as to when the English entered the wonderful walled city that was to become their capital, yet by following converging lines of evidence we may determine the point of time with almost certain accuracy. We have for this purpose (1) the chronicle of the conquests of the several branches of the Angle and Saxon peoples; (2) the British accounts and legends; (3) the traditional history, as given by such writers as Henry of Huntingdon and William of Malmesbury, of the succession of kings in the "Heptarchy."

(1) Up to *c.* 500 we have the conquests of Kent, Sussex, and Wessex, the first two confined to the present county limits, and the last with its centre at Winchester, only

reaching Sarum in 552, and striking north-east to Aylesbury and Bedford in 571. According to Dr. Guest and Mr. Green, the great fortress of London and its bridge up to this time barred the natural approach of the invaders up the Thames valley. Another horde, who became the East Saxons, had, in the meantime, effected a settlement in the county yet called after them. These reached Verulam about 560, for Gildas (*c.* 516 to 570) deplores the loss of that city, but says nothing of London. It was by the Wessex advance of 571 that the frontier between itself and Essex was defined; and as London, which is so near the boundary line, belonged (at a later time at least) to the latter, we may suppose that it had already before 571 been taken possession of by the East Saxons. Again, the men of Kent, in 568, attempted to press on over Surrey, but were beaten back by the men of Wessex. Mr. Green well suggests that this attempted advance was an immediate consequence of the reduction of London, which had hitherto held Kent back.

(2) The British legends given by Geoffrey of Monmouth refer to several incidents in London during the sixth century, culminating in the flight of Theon, its archbishop, in the second half of the century—Hovenden says in 586.

(3) Bede says that London was the metropolis of the East Saxons. Henry of Huntingdon tells us that Ella *founded* Sussex; Wessex was *founded* by Cerdic in the year 519; and

the kingdom of Essex—that is, of the East Saxons—was *founded* by Erchinwin, whose son Slede married the sister of Ethelbert, king of Kent. This Slede's son was Sebert, the first king of Essex converted to the Christian faith. Now we know that when Augustine's mission came in 597 Ethelbert was still reigning in Kent, and his nephew ruled in London when Mellitus brought the Gospel there in 604. If, then, we put the "foundation" of the kingdom of Essex by Sebert's grandfather some thirty or forty years before this time, we again reach the date of the probable occupation of London, which we may put provisionally about 570.

It was probably early in the sixth century that the Saxons began to get a footing in what became Essex, as in 527, according to Huntingdon, large bodies of men came from Germany and took possession of East Anglia, various chiefs of whom "contended for the occupation of different districts." We may suppose that Colchester first fell, then Verulam, and that London was entered only after its complete isolation, and as the culmination of the English Conquest of South Britain, just as was the case in the Norman Conquest exactly five hundred years later. All Celtic tradition looks back to London as the British capital. Dr. Rhys quotes a story from the Welsh Laws to the effect that "the nation of the Kymry, after losing the crown and sceptre of London and being driven out of England, assembled to decide who should be chief king."[23] In the story of Bran in the Mabinogion, which Celtic scholars say is untouched by any influence so late as Geoffrey's, it is told that the seven men journeying with the head of the Blessed Bran were told that Caswallawn the son of Beli "has conquered the Island of the Mighty and is crowned king in London."

Alfred's London.—In endeavouring to trace the topographical vestiges of London, as far as any sufficiently clear indications will allow, it will be found that we can easily carry back a great number of wards, streets, and churches to the century which followed the Conquest. More patient research allows of pushing still further a large number of "origins" to a time anterior to the Conquest, but subsequent to the Roman evacuation of the city. As the greatest of all London events in this space of time was the resettlement of the city by Alfred, less than two centuries before Duke William entered within its walls, and as London may readily be supposed to have altered very little in that time, we may well take the reign of the great king, who died exactly a thousand years ago, as the centre of gravity of the whole period, and the pages which follow might very well be called an account of London in the time of Alfred.

The strife with the Danes in the Thames valley raged from before the time of Alfred's birth. Stow and others have supposed that London was wrecked in 839, and lay waste until Alfred restored it; but it has been shown that the first attack on the city must have been in 842.[24] In 851 a great host of the pagans came with 350 ships to the mouth of the river Thames, and sacked Canterbury "and also the city of London, which lies on the confines of Essex and Middlesex, but the city belongs of right to Essex."[25] Before this time London had become subject to the overlordship of Mercia, and Behrtwulf the Mercian was killed in its defence.

There is a charter of Burgred, king of Mercia, relating to London, 857; in 872-74 the city was taken by Halfdan the Dane, and Burgred, king of Mercia, was ejected from his kingdom. In the coin room of the British Museum there is a remarkable coin which bears the legend ALFDENE RX ✠, and on the reverse the monogram of London which was later used by Alfred on his coins (Fig. 14). The obverse bears the same type as that used on the coins of Ceolwulf, whom Halfdan set up as his creature in Mercia: it cannot be doubted that Halfdan's coin was struck as a memorial of his wintering in London in 872-73, as described in the Anglo-Saxon Chronicle. All now was confusion, "down and up, and up and down, and dreadful," till at the peace of Wedmore, in 878, Alfred made a division of the country with the Danish leader Guthrum, by a boundary defined in the agreement as "upon the Thames along the Lea to its source, then right to Bedford and upon the Ouse to Watling Street." London thus fell to Alfred, who repaired it in 886 and made it again habitable, and gave it into the hands of his son-in-law Ethered.[26] Ethered was Ealdorman of Mercia, so London was still practically the Mercian capital, and remained so till the death of Ethered. London all the time was the chief city in the kingdom, but it then had to enter into competition with Winchester, the local capital of the dominating kingdom.

Fig. 14.—Coin of Halfdan with Monogram of London.

In 893 there was a fresh attack by the Danes, but they were defeated outside the city by the men of London, led by Ethered. In the account of this raid from the south coast through Farnham and northwards across the Thames, as given in Ethelweard's Chronicle, the Danes are said to have been besieged on Thorney Isle (*Thornige Insula*), the site of the abbey of Westminster. The Danes then passed eastward and took up positions at Mersea, Shoebury, and probably Welbury, near the Lea, in all of which places there are traces of earthworks.[27]

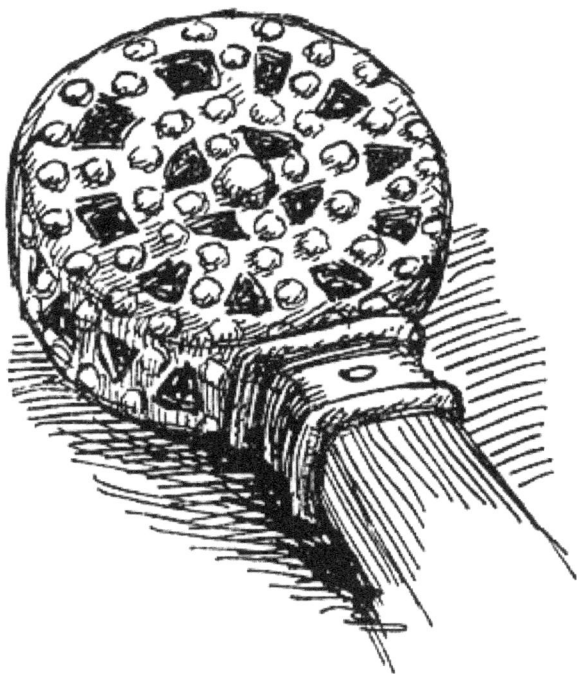

Fig. 15.—Saxon Swordhilt.

Since the resettlement of London in 886 there has been no interruption of the continuity of city life and customs, and it is very probable that some of the institutions shaped by the great organiser, whom William Morris called the one man of genius who has ever ruled in England, remain to this day.

CHAPTER II

RIVERS AND FORDS

And dream of London, small and white and clean,
The clear Thames bordered by its gardens green.
The Earthly Paradise.

The city of London, when the Roman garrison was withdrawn from its walls, occupied two hills on the north river-bank, between which ran the Walbrook. The river, which still retains its British or pre-British name of Thames,[28] spread, as may be seen from a geological map, over wide tracts of morass, which at an early time began to be protected by embankments, which are "no less than 50 feet above low water, and, counting side creeks, 300 miles long."

The Chronicle of Bermondsey records of a flood in 1294-95:—"Then was made the great breach at Retherhith; and it overflowed the plain of Bermundeseye and the precinct of Tothill." The French Chronicle, written some two generations afterwards, shows that this was still remembered as "Le Breche." Edward I. at once issued a mandate that the banks from Lambeth to Greenwich should be viewed and repaired. Stow, under Westminster, says that in 1236 the river "overflowing the banks made the Woolwich marshes all on a sea" and flowed into Westminster Hall; and again in 1242 "drowned houses and fields by the space of six miles" on the Lambeth side. In 1448 "the water brake in out of Thames beside Lymeost and in another place."[29] Howel (1657) writes: "The Thames often inounds the bankes about London, which makes the grounds afterwards more fertile."

Howe Brute buylded London/ & cal
led this londe Brytayne/and Scotlon=
de Albyne/and Walys Camber.

London.

BRute & his men wente forthe and
sawe about in dyuers places/whe
re that they myght fynde a good place &
couenable/ that they myght make a cy=
te for hym & for his folke. And so at the
laste they came by a fayre Ryuer þ is cal
led Tamyps/& there Brute began to bu=
ylde a fayre Cyte/and lette calle it newe
Troy/in mynde & remembraunce of the

*Fig. 16.—Earliest Printed View of
London from the Chronicle of
Englonde, Pynson 1510.*

The embankments seem to have been called walls. The names of Bermondsey Wall and Wapping Wall still survive opposite one another; and "wall" enters into the names of several places bordering on the river, as Millwall and Blackwall, and St. Peter's on the Wall, at Bradwell, Essex, where the north bank ends. At Lambeth Pennant noted that the name Narrow Walls occurred. The general opinion is that these banks are either Roman or pre-Roman work. Wren thought Roman.[30]

Before the locks were made on the river the tide ran up past Richmond to near the inlet of the Mole.[31] London held the jurisdiction over the river from Yanlet to Staines from the twelfth century at least. The limit at either end is marked by a "London Stone."

FitzStephen calls the river "the great fish-bearing Thames." Howel in his *Londinopolis* says: "The Thames water useth to be as clear and pellucid as any such great river in the world, except after a land flood, when 'tis usual to take up haddocks with one's hand beneath the Bridge." Harrison (1586) writes: "What should I speak of the fat and sweet salmons daily taken in this stream, and that in such plenty after the time of smelt be past, as no river in Europe is able to exceed it." Even in the last century stray whales and porpoises used to find their way up on the tide. The Saxon foredwellers must have had their fill of fish. Even the

Thames swans can be traced back to the fourteenth century in a document relating to the Tower.[32] William Dunbar in 1501 wrote:—

> Above all ryvers thy Ryver hath renowne
> Whose beryall stremys, pleasant and preclare
> Under thy lusty wallys runneth down
> Where many a Swanne doth swymme with winges fare.

Stow's account of the smaller streams "serving the city" is the most unfortunate in the classic survey, and entirely untrustworthy.

In the hollow some distance west of Ludgate was a tidal inlet; a part of its bed has (in 1900) just been exposed in New Bridge Street; the name Fleet, indeed, must express a tidal creek. Early in the twelfth century the district beyond it is called *ultra Fletam*.[33] The inlet gave its name to the bridge and street passing over it from Ludgate. Rishanger calls the latter Fleet-Bridge Street. Henry II. gave to the Templars a site for a mill *super Fletam Juxta Castelum Bainard*, and all the course of the water of Fleet and a messuage *juxta pontem de Flete*. A messuage on the Fleet was also given to them by Gervase of Cornhill, *Teintarius*, and this record is interesting as giving us the calling of the great Londoner treated of so fully by Mr. Round.[34] Gervase was one of the most important personalities in twelfth-century London, and it is not commonly realised that members of the crafts so early held power.

Into the Fleet, down the still well-marked valley by Farringdon Road, ran a stream sometimes called the Fleet River; it is plotted on some of the earlier maps, and its course has been traced in detail by Mr. Waller.[35] In an agreement as to the land of the nunnery at Clerkenwell, made at the end of the twelfth century, this stream is unmistakably called the Hole-burn; its valley ran north and south by Clerkenwell, and the river and gardens of the Hospitallers of Jerusalem are said to have been upon it.[36] It gave its name to Holborn Bridge and to some extra-mural cottages near by, on the road which passed over it. The modern name should mean Hole-burn-Bridge Street, just as Fleet Street meant Fleet-Bridge Street. Holeburn Street is found in 1249. [37] Cottages at "Holeburne," which had existed in the time of the Confessor, are mentioned in Domesday, and we may conclude that the Holeburn and Fleet had these names not only in King Edward's day, but in Alfred's. The upper part of the stream was also called Turnmill brook; it was the mill stream of London.

Stow also gives the name of the River of Wells to this western stream just described, saying: "That it was of old called of the Wells may be proved thus: William the Conqueror in his charter to the College of St. Martin le Grand hath these words, 'I do give and grant ... all the land and the Moor without Cripplegate, on either side of the postern, that is to say, from the north corner of the wall as the river of the Wells, there near running, departeth the same moor from the wall, unto the running water which entereth the city.'"[38] He goes on to say that the stream (Hole-burn) was still called Wells in the time of Edward I., citing the Parliament and Patent Rolls of 1307; but on referring to the calendars of these documents I find that this name of Wells appears in neither. The first speaks of "the water-course of Fleet running under the bridge of Holburn," and the second of them calls it "the Fleet River from Holburn Bridge to the Thames." Moreover, the Hole-burn was far away from the north corner of the city wall by Cripplegate, and the land granted cannot have extended all the way to the present Farringdon Road (the bed of the old stream) and have included Smithfield. The land of "Crepelesgate," taken by William Rufus and restored to St. Martin's by Henry I., is probably the same, and to-day it may be represented by the parish of St. Giles. Surely the whole construction of the passage requires that the north-west angle of the walls should be the western limit of the land granted.

The Conqueror's Latin charter is given in Dugdale, and in the passage used by Stow the stream is spoken of as *rivulus foncium*. Mr. Stevenson, in publishing a Saxon version of the same charter 1068 A.D.,[39] shows that *rivulus foncium* was

51

a translation of the O.E. *Wylrithe*, meaning a small stream (*rithe*) issuing from a spring (*wyl*). This "Well-brook"[40] must surely have been intended, not for the western stream at all, but for the upper part of the "broke" running into the "burh" directly afterwards mentioned in the charter, the present Walbrook. Outside the walls the stream possibly ran in a west-to-east direction, and so formed the north boundary of the property against the moor.

Mr. Stevenson appears not to have been of this view himself, as he speaks of the Walbrook as "probably nameless" when the charter was written; but he points out that it was called Walebroc in a charter of Wulfnoth (1114-33)— "probably the Wulfnoth whose name is recorded in St. Mary Woolnoth." This is a Ramsey charter (in Rolls series), and the terms are most precise by which Wulfnoth of Walebroc, London, sold a piece of land in Walebroc, "whence he was called Wulfnoth of Walebroc," with a house of stone and a shop, for ten pounds of pence.[41]

St. John "super Walebroc" is mentioned about the same time in the St. Paul's documents, and that Walbrook was then a proper name of some antiquity seems to be conclusively proved by Geoffrey of Monmouth's legend that it was called after Gallus by the Britons, "and in the Saxon Gallembourne." Altogether it can hardly be doubted that the Wyl- of the charter represents the modern Wal- in Walbrook.[42]

Within the walls the Walbrook ran right through the midst of the city from north to south, and divided the eastern wards from the western. It remained an open stream well into the Middle Ages; in 1286 an order was given to cleanse it "from the Moor of London to the Thames." Its course is well defined by three churches, St. John's, St. Stephen's (formerly on a different site to the west, Stow), and St. Mildred's, all "super Walbrook." St. Margaret Lothbury also stood above it on vaults. Its relation to the present street is made clear in a document of 1291 regarding a tenement "between the course of the Walbrook towards the west, and Walbrook Street towards the east."[43] The arch under which it entered the city through the wall seems to have been discovered. Roach Smith describes this opening thus: "Opposite Finsbury Circus, at a depth of 19 feet, a well-turned Roman arch was discovered, at the entrance of which on the Finsbury side were iron bars placed apparently to restrain the sedge and weeds from choking the passage."[44]

The bed of the brook has frequently been found in city excavations, and its course has been laid down by Mr. T. E. Price.[45] It was of course crossed by many bridges; in 1291 there was an inquiry held as to the repair of one of them near the "tenement of Bokerelesbery."[46] This stream was probably the first water supply of London, and it must have been a most important factor in the division of the wards and the laying out of the streets.

53

The Langbourne described by Stow is entirely mythical. As he named Holborn from a merely supposititious "Old-burn" running east and west, so also his Lang-burn has its only origin, as will be shown, in the corruption of a name (see p. 132). Here I need only say that its supposed bed occupies high ground, and no evidence of it has been found in excavations. Mr. Price points out that Stow himself allowed that the name was the only sign of it, and adds that the levels demonstrate that no such stream can ever have flowed there; indeed, excavations have shown that its supposed course was one of the most populous parts of the early city.[47]

Stow connects with it still another equally mythical stream, the Share-burne, on the site of Sherborne Lane, but I find this called Shitteborwe in 1272, and the last syllable must be "bury," not "burn."

Fords.—The best account of the Thames fords is given by Dr. Guest.[48] Cæsar tells us that the river called Thames was passable on foot only in one place, and this ford was defended against him by stakes. Bede says that the remains of the stakes were to be seen there "to this very day." Camden suggested that the site of this ford was Coway Stakes, near Walton; King Alfred, however, in an addition he made to Orosius, says that Cæsar, after defeating the "Bryttas in Cent-land," fought again "nigh the Temese by the ford called

Welinga-ford." Wallingford, where the Icknield Way crossed the river, was certainly the chief ford below Oxford. Dr. Guest showed that a place near Coway Stakes is called Halliford, and argued that although a Roman army, that of Claudius, may have crossed at Wallingford, Cæsar's passage of the river was at the stakes, and the two passages of the river came to be confused in the tradition. The general argument is too subtle to go into here, but it is less than convincing to make Bede's account of a ford where stakes yet remained in the river apply to Cæsar and the Coway Stakes, while Alfred's applied to Wallingford and the army of Claudius, especially as we may suppose that a principal ford would be fortified if a lesser one were. According to the Anglo-Saxon Chronicle, Sweyn's army passed the river at Wallingford; here William the Conqueror also crossed; and here too it seems likely that the English invaders also first crossed.[49]

Another place nearer to London which is named from a ford is Brentford, but Dr. Guest thought that the ford so named was over the Brent instead of the Thames. He allows that the English army here twice crossed over the Thames in 1016, as recorded in the Chronicle, but argues that there was only a "shallow" in the Thames at this point, and that the *ford* was over the Brent. William of Malmesbury, however, seems to have anticipated all this by saying very distinctly "the ford called Brentford" and the "ford at Brentford" when speaking of the crossings of the Thames in 1016. Gough in his edition of Camden says that the Thames was easily passed here at low water.

Of a ford at Westminster, which from a mere unsubstantial hypothesis has swollen into quite a big myth in the pages of Sir W. Besant, there is not a scrap of evidence. There was, however, throughout the Middle Age a ferry here, and the name still survives in Horseferry Road. The Roman bridge at Staines (*Pontes*) may be the one, the existence of which is implied in the Anglo-Saxon Chronicle for 1013, and in 1009 we are told that the army went over the river at Staines.[50] In the Middle Ages there was a bridge between Staines and London on the river at Kingston, and Horsley thought that Cæsar crossed by a ford here.

CHAPTER III

ROADS AND THE BRIDGE

Upon thy lusty brigge of pylers white
Been merchauntis full royall to behold:
Upon thy stretis goeth many a semely Knyght
Arrayit in velvet gownes and cheynes of gold.
William Dunbar.

Roads.—The Roman roads of the Antonine Itinerary which affect London are: Iter 2, the great road from Canterbury to London and St. Albans and beyond (the Watling Street); Iter 5, London to Colchester, and from thence to Lincoln; Iter 6, London to Lincoln, starting by the Watling Street; Iter 7, from Chichester through Silchester and passing the river at Staines (*Pontes*), through Brentford to London.[51]

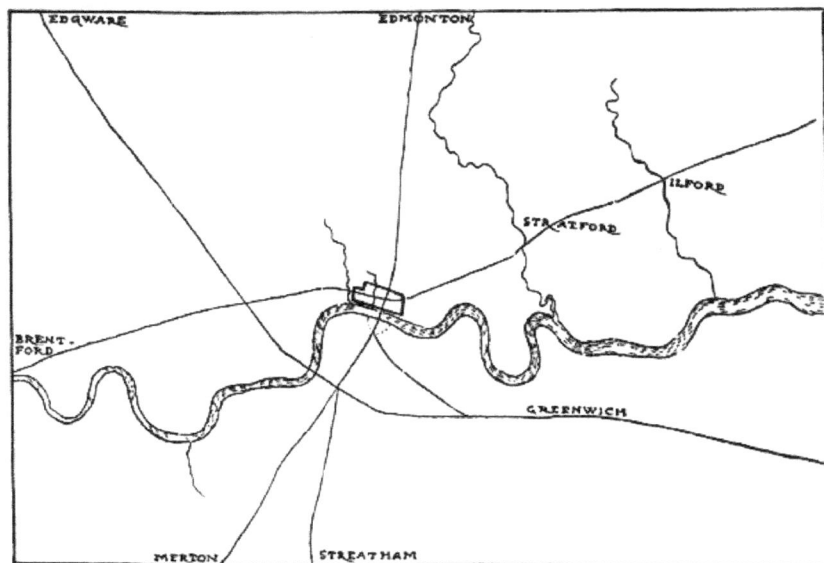

Fig. 17.—London and the Roman Roads.

In the (so-called) Laws of Edward the Confessor, a clause treats of the King's peace on the four great roads, *Watlingestrete, Fosse, Hekenildestrete,* and *Ermingestrete,* two of which are said to run through the length of the realm and two across.[52] In the British legends given by Geoffrey, the making of these roads is ascribed to Belinus, and they are said to have been paved with stone and mortar; the four are evidently the chief Roman roads in the island. The identification of the Watling Street is certain, for Bede says that St. Albans was called Watlingcester, and Saxon charters show that Hampstead and Paddington were on it;

it is the modern Edgware Road. Henry of Huntingdon tells us that the Watling Street ran from the south-east to the north-west, and that Erming Street ran from north to south. Higden, in the fourteenth century, says that the Watling Street began at Dover and passed through Kent and "over the Thames at London, west of Westminster," then to St. Albans, Dunstable, Stratford, etc.[53] Camden says: "The Roman road commonly called Watling Street leads straight to London over Hampstead Heath, whence is a fine prospect of a beautiful city and cultivated country."

The best reasons that can be given for the position of the Watling Street are that it was first formed before London became of much importance, that it avoided the great Essex forest, and passed over the Thames at a point convenient for a ferry on its way to and from Dover.

Such prehistoric traffic as there was, by a sort of commercial drainage, gathering together in a stream directed on Dover, must have tended to pass the river with the least possible deflection. Whether or not the great Watling Street is entirely of Roman date, a ferry at Westminster may have superseded the Brent-ford. The actual passage was probably from Tothill Street to Stangate on the south side of the river: "Stangate" is still used as the name of a Roman road in the North by Hadrian's Great Wall. After the Palace of Westminster was built, the ferry must have been diverted by the Horseferry Road, and Higden may refer to this position.

Clark suggests that "the Tothill" was a Saxon military mound, as such mounds are sometimes called "toot-hills"; if so, it was a protection overlooking the Watling Street, and may very well have been a mound raised by Alfred in the Danish struggle.[54] "Le Tothull" is mentioned in 1250, when Henry III. granted the Abbey to hold a fair there. Hollar's view shows a mound. The Tothill was common ground, and everything points to its having been formerly a defensive work. The west gate of Westminster was "towards Tothill" (1350), and Vincent Square now represents Tothill Fields. The Lang ditch, which nearly surrounded Westminster, and which can be traced back to the twelfth century, was probably a dyke of defence.

Stukeley, writing in 1722, when material evidence was not so hard to find, says that the Watling Street crossed over another Roman road (now Oxford Street), which passed by the back of Kensington into the great road to Brentford and Staines, "a Roman road all the way." The Watling Street then went across the end of Hyde Park, and by St. James's Park to the street near Palace Yard called the Wool Staple, and crossed to Stangate on the opposite side of the river. The southward continuation of the road then passed over St. George's Fields to Deptford and Blackheath; "a small portion of the ancient way pointing to (or from) Westminster Abbey is now the common road: ... from the top of Shooters' Hill the direction of the road is very plain both ways: ... beyond the hill it is very straight as far as the ken reaches: on Blackheath is a tumulus."

From the Watling Street, on Blackheath, was obtained the first prospect of London, where travellers during the Middle Age paused, as visitors to Rome paused on their way only half a century agone. The mayor with all the crafts of the city, in 1415, rode out thus far to meet Henry V. returning from France.

> The King from Eltham sone he cam,
> Hys prisenors with hym dede brynge,
> And to the Blak-heth ful sone he cam.
> He saw London withoughte lesynge;
> Heil, ryall London, seyde our Kyng,
> Crist the Kepe evere from care.—Lydgate.

In his letter to Wren Dr. Woodward says that in several places lying near by in a line, particularly on this side of Shooters' Hill, where the country is low, there remained a raised highway 40 feet wide and 4 feet high. According to Allen's history a portion of the Roman way leading to Stangate was found just north of Newington Church in 1824.

Stukeley thought that the west-to-east road, over the present Oxford Street, originally passed to the north of London into Essex (by Old Street), "because London was not then considerable, but in a little time Holborn was struck out from it, entering the city at Newgate, and so to London-Stone, the *Lapis Milliaris*, and hence the reason why the name of Watling Street is still preserved in the city."

There can be no doubt that Stukeley's account of the Roman roads is generally true, but the theory of the great road by Old Street seems unlikely, although the latter is quite certainly a Roman way, and was called Ealde Street in the twelfth century.[55] The Roman road has been found 11 feet below the surface, together with Roman coins.[56] There cannot be a doubt that, in late Roman days at least, the great west-to-east road passed through the city and by the Mile End Road through Stratford and the other places named from "street" to Chelmsford and Colchester. Besides the great Roman roads there were of course many local ways. The High Street from Aldersgate to Islington, also mentioned in the twelfth century,[57] is probably, like the gate through which it passed, Roman too. Stow's hypothesis that Old Street branched away from the top of Aldersgate Street seems best to meet the case. Stukeley's suggestion about the naming of "Watling Street" in the city, which has been so embroidered upon by recent writers, seems, as we shall show (p. 150), to be a mistake.

It is asserted in a fourteenth-century document quoted by Lysons that the great east road passed the Lea by Old Ford before Matilda built Bow Bridge; but this has no weight in excluding the road by Aldgate against the evidence of the great road itself. The name Stratford is mentioned as Strachford in a charter of the Conqueror.[58] In the life of St. Erkenwald given in the Golden Legend, it is said that his body was brought to London from Barking through Stratford after a miraculous passage of the Lea. There *may* have been a road by Old Street and Old Ford, but there *must* have been a road by Holborn and Whitechapel through Newgate and Aldgate.[59]

The branch from the great Watling Street to the city, by Tyburn and St. Andrew's Holborn, is described in a charter giving in Saxon the boundaries of Westminster, dated 951, but not original. This charter, even if forged, can hardly be later than the era of the Conquest, when the coterminous manor of Eya was given to the Abbey by Geoffrey de Mandeville; and the names found in it must then have been of immemorial antiquity. Mr. Stevenson, in a recent criticism of the document, accepts it as genuine and proposes the date 971.[60] It reads: "First up from the Thames along Merfleet to Pollenstock, so to Bulinga Fen, and along the old ditch to Cuforde. From Cuforde along the Tyburn to the *Here Straet*, and by it to the Stock of St. Andrew's Church, then in London Fen south to Midstream of Thames, and by land

63

and strand to the Merfleet." *Here Street* is the usual Saxon name for a Roman road, but it will be convenient to use it in this case as a proper name.

The stream of Tyburn crossed Oxford Street just west of Stratford Place, and ran through the Green Park, and so to the west of Westminster. Cufford I find again, *temp.* Edward I., as in, or near, the *Campis de Eya*—now Hyde Park and St. James's.[61] This Cowford was probably where Piccadilly "dip" crosses the Tyburn valley. A bridge is shown here in Faithorne's map. The Here Street or military road is of course Oxford Street and Holborn, and London-Fen is the Fleet valley.[62]

The manor of Tyburn appears in Domesday. There can be no doubt as to the identification of the Here Street, for a document of 1222 gives as the boundaries of St. Margaret's, Westminster, the water of Tyburn running to the Thames and the *Strata Regia* extending to London past the garden of St. Giles [in-the-Fields], and Roman remains have been found in Holborn. The Here Street has been traced between Silchester and Staines through Egham, and on this side of Staines, not far from Ashford, it has been found. [63] An under road to Kensington, etc., by Knightsbridge must also have been ancient. Knightsbridge is named in a twelfth-century charter, and it seems to be the same as the Kingsbridge in a charter of the Confessor.[64]

From the fact that the Antonine Itinerary gives two routes to Lincoln,—one round to the west by the Watling Street, and one to the east by Colchester,—it seems probable that the direct Erming Street was made in the later Roman era.

The best critical account of the four Roman ways is in *Origines Celticæ* and the *Archæological Journal* for 1857, in which Dr. Guest, working from charters, verifies their position. He considers that the portion of the Erming Street between London and Huntingdon was not a Roman paved road, although "it must have existed in the days of Edgar, and perhaps as early as the times of Offa." "Tracks of an ancient causey may still be found alongside the turnpike road which leads from London to Royston," beyond which the road passes straight on over the fens to a place called Ermingford in Domesday and Earmingaford in a charter of Edgar. To the south of London he lays down a "Stone Street" from Chichester through Bignor (Roman villa) and Dorking. In vol. ix. of *Archæologia*, Bray, the co-author of the *History of Surrey*, traces this "Roman road through Sussex and Surrey to London." "That there was a great road from Arundel which ran north and north-east to London is very certain, considerable remains of it being now (1788) visible in many places." Another road from the south seems to have passed through Croydon and Streatham, which in a charter of the Confessor is called Stratham.[65] Near Ockley the former was called "Stone Street Causeway," and Camden speaks of it as "the old military road of the Romans called Stone Street." It was "some 30 feet broad and some 4 or 5 feet thick of stones." Considerable vestiges of this Roman road may even now be traced on the Ordnance Survey; approaching London it evidently passed through Epsom, Ewell, Merton, Tooting, and Clapham. Here then we have a great road from Chichester through Surrey over London Bridge and by Stamford Hill to Lincoln—the Erming Street. It seems impossible that such a work could have been undertaken in the time of the "Heptarchy," and it must be a Roman road made subsequently to the Antonine Itinerary.

When London Bridge was built, or when a regular ferry over the Thames was established on this line, a new connection with the Canterbury Road (Watling Street) was evidently called for, and this link was provided by Kent Street (now Great Dover Street). Bagford, in his letter to Hearne, says that the Roman approach and military way led along Kent Street on the left-hand side, "and pointed directly to Dowgate by the Bishop of Winchester's stairs, which to this day is called Stone Street." I cannot, however, accept the inference as to the name Stone Street in this place, as it ran directly through what was Winchester Palace, where, as old views show, there cannot have been a street in the Middle Ages. The highway from the bridge going southwards really ran straight through the borough (Burh or South-work), and deflected on to Kent Street at St. George's Church, which stood here early in the twelfth century (see Southwark, below, p. 110).

The English invaders came up the Watling Street and were unsuccessfully met at Crayford. At Ockley on the Stone Street there was a great battle with the Danes. William the Conqueror, after the battle of Hastings, took Dover and Canterbury and came to London by the Watling Street; then burning Southwark, but not venturing to assault the walled city, he moved down the Stone Street and across to Farnham and Wallingford, and then north-east, by the Icknield Way, and so commanded the northern Watling Street and Erming Street and cut off retreat. A recent study of his route made from Domesday Book makes him pass through Camberwell, Merton, Guildford, and Farnham. Then crossing the river by both Wallingford and Streatley, he approached London by Little Berkhamstead, Enfield, and Tottenham.[66]

A final consideration of the roads in relation to the city shows two great routes: (1) from west to east, through Staines to Colchester; and (2) from south to north, from Chichester to Lincoln. These roads, entering the city by Holborn and the bridge, and issuing by Aldgate and Bishopsgate, were throughout the Middle Ages the great market streets, and their intersection at Leadenhall formed the "Carfax" of London.

The best elucidation of the names of the roads we have been concerned with is given by Dr. Guest. One is the street of the Ermings or Fenmen, who gave their name to places on its course. The Icknield Way, which he gives good reasons for thinking was a British road, led to the district of the Iceni (compare Dr. Rhys, *Celtic Folklore*, p. 676). The Watling Street he supposes to be the Irishmen's road, from Welsh *Gwythel—Goidel—*Irishman. These derivations seem to be a little over symmetrical. Other roads than that through St. Albans were called Watling Street, which almost seems to be a generic term, just as in Wales the Roman ways are called Sarn Helen. In the story of Maxen Wledig (Maximus Emperor) we are told that the Empress Helen made the roads. It is probably a similar legend where Florence says that old tradition had it that London was walled by Helen. Florence says that the Watling Street was called so from the sons of King Weatla: Can this be a corruption of Wledig, or can the reference be to the British prince Guithlin, who seems to have been in power about the time of the coming of the Saxons?[67]

Horsley and others have thought that these roads were laid down for the most part immediately after the Roman conquest by Claudius, and there can hardly be a doubt of their early existence when we consider the great works of Agricola as far off as the Roman Wall.[68] Moreover, one or two milestones which have been found bear the name of Hadrian. The antiquity of our place-names, roads, and bridges is well brought out in a seventh-century charter to Chertsey Abbey. The land boundary, beginning at the mouth of the Wey, passed by Weybridge, then by the mill-stream to the old Here Street and along it to Woburn Bridge, etc. This Here Street is doubtless the present road on the south bank of the Thames; it probably led from Southwark, through Clapham—called Cloppaham in the ninth century—by Wandsworth, where was a church in the tenth century, and by Kingston, the royal town and crowning place of the later Saxon kings.[69]

The Bridge.—We hear of the existence of the bridge about seventy years after Alfred's time in connection with the punishment of a woman who was to be taken and "a-drownded at Lundene-brigce."[70] In a poem on Holy Olaf the King of Norway, by a contemporary, he is said to have broken down London Bridge in an attack on the Danes in the interest of Ethelred about 1014.[71] It is curious that the English Chronicles do not speak of this, and it is difficult to fit in, but in any case the story is almost contemporary.

An extended but later account of the incident is given in the *Heimskringla*: "Now first they made for London and went up the Thames with the host of the ships, but the Danes held the city. On the other side of the river there is a great Cheaping-town called Southwark (Sudurvirke); there the Danes had great arrayal; they had dug great dykes, on the inner side whereof they had built a wall of turf and stone.... A bridge was there across the river betwixt the city and Southwark, so broad that waggons might be driven past each other thereover. On the bridge were made strongholds, both castles and bulwarks, looking down stream, so high that they reached a man above his waist; but under the bridge were pales stuck into the bottom of the river. And when an onset was made the host stood on the bridge all along it and warded it. King Ethelred was mickle mind-sick how he was to win the bridge." King Olaf made wooden shelters over his boats, "and the host of the Northmen rowed right up under the bridge and lashed cables round the pales which upheld the bridge, and they fell to their oars and rowed down stream as hard as they might, ... and the pales having broken from under it, the bridge broke down by reason thereof; ... and after this they made an onset on Southwark and won it. And when the townsfolk [of London] saw that the river Thames was won, so that they might not hinder ships from faring up into the land, they were afeared, and gave up the town and took King Ethelred in. So says Ottar the Swart:—

O battle-bold, the cunning
Of Yggs storm! Yet thou brakest

Down London Bridge: it happed thee
To win the land of snakes there."

This verse is sometimes translated so as to read "London Bridge is broken down" in the first line, like the well-known children's song; but there have been many breakings down since the time of Olaf, and it is unnecessary to force such a remote origin for the ditty. As to the bridge itself, the account just given as to its being of wood agrees with the fact that no piers seem to have been preserved when it was rebuilt in the twelfth century. That it should have been fortified agrees with contemporary events, for Charles the Bald had built a fortified bridge at Paris to stop the pirates going up the river.

The bridge, as we have seen, was required by the Roman roads, and must have been of Roman origin. Roach Smith, indeed, even considered that it might have been the bridge by which Claudius is said to have crossed the river, and points out that the Itinerary shows that bridges were not uncommon in Britain.[72] "This presumptive evidence" [as to London Bridge being of early Roman origin] "is supported by recent discoveries. Throughout the entire line of the old bridge, the bed of the river was found to contain ancient wooden piles; and when these piles, subsequently to the erection of the new bridge (about 1835), were pulled up to deepen the channel of the river, *many thousands* of

Roman coins, with abundance of Roman tiles and pottery, were discovered; and immediately beneath some of the central piles, brass medallions of Aurelius, Faustina, and Commodus. All these remains are indicative of a bridge. The enormous quantity of Roman coins may be accounted for by the well-known practice of the Romans to use them to perpetuate the memory of their conquests and public works. They may have been deposited either upon the building or repair of the bridge. The great rarity of the medallions is corroborative of this opinion." Many bronzes and other works of art were also found.[73]

I incline to the view that the bridge may with greatest probability be assigned to the century when the Romans were consolidating their work in Britain, from the arrival of Agricola in A.D. 78. Within this period falls the date of the earliest medals found and the great building age of Hadrian, who reared the "Roman Wall." It is tempting to suggest that the fine head of Hadrian, in 1863 found in the Thames, may have formed a part of a statue placed on the bridge to commemorate his visit. Bronze has always been too valuable a material for the head to have been wilfully cast away. Moreover, we have evidences of two bridges by the Roman Wall which were the work of Hadrian. That at Newcastle, called after him, Pons Ælii, had a history curiously parallel with London Bridge, for it gave way to a mediæval bridge in 1248, which was destroyed in the flood of 1771. During the rebuilding parts of the Roman structure were found. Near Hexham, where the line of the wall crosses the North Tyne, there are still vestiges of a bridge which seems to have lasted down to 1771; it has three piers of masonry, having angular cut-waters up-stream. The spans were 35 feet, the piers about 16 feet transversely; the roadway was about 20 feet wide; at the ends, standing over the masonry abutments, were towers through which the roadway passed. "The platform of this bridge was undoubtedly of timber. Several of the stones which lie on the ground have grooves in them for admitting the spars. No arch-stones have been found."[74]

Old London Bridge crossed the river just east of the existing bridge. Stow thought that the original bridge was still farther east, because St. Botolph's Port is mentioned in connection with the bridge in a charter of the Conqueror. Notwithstanding that this conjecture was disproved so fully when the old bridge was destroyed, the theory still appears in standard books and on maps which profess to represent Old London.

CHAPTER IV

THE WALLS, GATES, AND QUAYS

On board his bark he goes straight to London, beneath
the bridge; his merchandise he there shows, his cloths of silk
smoothes and opens out.—*Roman de Tristan.*

Walls.—The walls and gates of London are frequently
mentioned incidentally by the chroniclers of the Saxon
period. In the charter given by William the Conqueror to
St. Martin's le Grand, the city guarded by them is called the
Burh, and the defences themselves are called Burhwealles.
Their complete circuit can be accurately traced from existing
remnants, old plans and records. Some years ago a fragment
of the east wall of Roman date was found, which still exists
a few yards east of the south-east angle of the Keep of the
Tower, at a point which must be very near to the original
junction with the south or river wall, which probably ran in
the line of the present south wall of the inner ward of the
Tower. The city wall passed north by Aldgate to the N.E.
angle; then on the north by Bishopsgate and Cripplegate to
the N.W. angle, and, after making an inset by Aldersgate,
it formed another N.W. angle; thence it passed straight
south by Ludgate to the river. It was only at the end of the
thirteenth century that the south-west angle of the city was

extended to take in Blackfriars. Ample evidence of Roman workmanship has been found for the whole extent of the north and east sides, but until recently some have doubted whether any remains of Roman date had been found on the west; a portion, however, was discovered between Warwick Square and Old Bailey some twenty years ago, and in 1900 other portions were found at Newgate Prison. Still earlier in 1843, as Roach Smith pointed out in *Collectanea Antiqua* (vol. i.), a portion of the city wall was found near Apothecaries' Hall in Playhouse Yard. It was 10 feet thick, and the stones were bedded in mortar mixed with powdered brick. In the walls of some part of the old Blackfriars buildings found in 1900, I noticed that a considerable quantity of the small cubical Roman stones had been re-used in the Friary after the destruction of the south portion of the western wall of the city. Roach Smith pointed out that the steep fall in the ground just south of the *Times* office and St. Andrew's Church showed that the river wall passed along here. There is no doubt that Alfred's London included the whole of the Roman city with the exception of the Blackfriars extension.

Fig. 18.—Roman Wall of London.

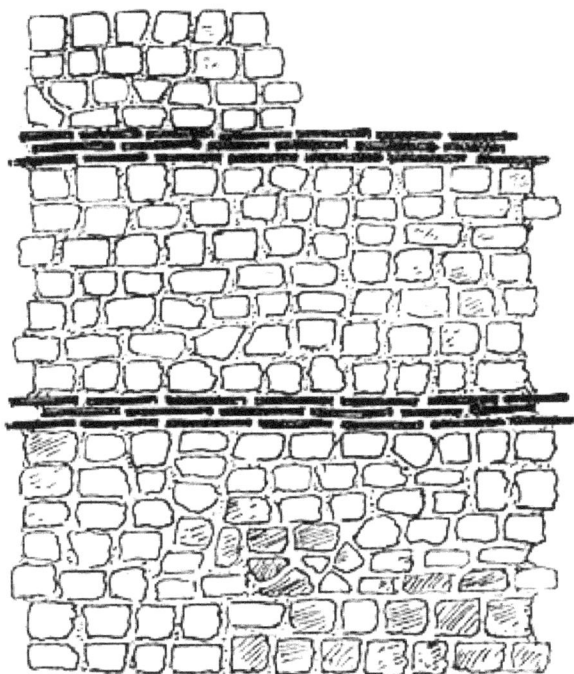

Fig. 19.—Detail of Roman Wall of London.

The city wall seems to have been uniformly built throughout its circuit of small stones, 6 or 7 inches square on the face, bonded about every sixth course with two or three courses of large flat tiles nearly 18 inches by 12 inches, and 1½ inches thick. The core was rough rubble; it was about 8 to 10 feet thick and probably 20 to 25 feet high. FitzStephen (*c.* 1180) describes it as "the high and great wall of the city having seven double gates and towered to the north at intervals; it was walled and towered in like manner on the

south, but the Thames has thrown down those walls." There
is evidence for a square Roman wall-tower having existed in
Houndsditch, and for others, semicircular in form. It would
always have had, as we know it had at a later time, a walk
all round, a parapet, and battlements. A part of the late wall
which still shows the walk and battlements is yet in London
Wall. The turrets (of the later wall at least) were higher than
the wall.

Fig. 20.—From the Common Seal. Reverse, enlarged, 1224.

According to Stow, the ditch of the city wall was begun
in 1211, and the same writer, speaking of the Walbrook
entering the city, as mentioned in the Conqueror's charter,
adds "before there was any ditch." This is a mistake, for
notices of Houndsditch appear before 1211, and the name
is used in the *Liber Trinitatis* in a way that infers its existence
before 1125. A few years ago an excavation at Aldersgate

exposed a complete section of the ditch outside the wall. It was 14 feet deep, 35 feet wide at bottom, and 75 feet wide at the top of the sloping sides. The top of the inner slope was 10 feet from the wall. This is drawn and described in vol. lii. of *Archæologia*, and a comparison subsequently made with the ditch at Silchester showed that, like it, it was certainly of Roman work. In each there was found a raised foundation in the bed of the ditch for a trestle bridge crossing from the gate (Fig. 21).

After the ruins of the fire (of five or six years ago) at Cripplegate were cleared away, it was evident that the basements of the houses in the street running north and south outside the west end of St. Giles's churchyard, by the angle bastion of the wall which still stands there, were built in the old ditch. A length of embanked stream which fed the ditch ran by the east of Finsbury Circus.[75] It is shown in the so-called Aggas plan.

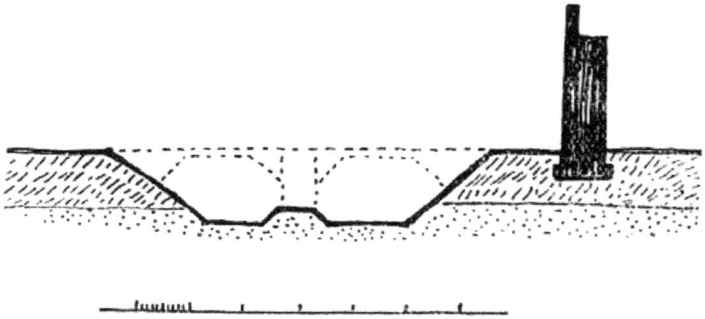

Fig. 21.—Section of Roman Wall and Ditch.

Many considerations suggest the likelihood that the first Roman walled city was smaller in extent than it became at a later time. Roach Smith thought that this earlier city was confined to the east side of the Walbrook, the approach from London Bridge forming its centre. The great wall, according to him, was "probably a work of the later days of the Romano-British period." With this view J. R. Green agrees, and argues that the wall was built in haste under Theodosius, when the attacks of Picts and Saxons made walls necessary for the security of British towns.[76] Henry of Huntingdon, writing early in the twelfth century, tells us that "tradition says that Helen, the illustrious daughter of Britain, surrounded London with the wall which is still standing."

Gates.—Opposite the entrance to the city by the bridge was the *North Gate*, called Bishopsgate. According to Geoffrey of Monmouth, Cæsar's sword "Yellow Death" was buried here with a Briton who had been slain by it. This legend is at least enough to show that the gate was ancient at the beginning of the twelfth century. Bishopsgate is mentioned in Domesday: "The canons of St. Paul's have *ad portam episcopi* ten cottages as in the time of King Edward." Outside the gate the Erming Street stretched away to the north over the moor.

The *East Gate*—Aldgate (generally written Algate or Alegate)—is mentioned in the foundation charters of Holy Trinity Priory in 1108. Stow says he found it named in a charter given by King Edgar to the Cnihten Gild, but it seems that he founded this on a later legend which professed to recite the terms of such a charter. However, the Saxon Chronicle, giving an account of the dispute between the Confessor and Godwine in 1052, says that some of the Earl's party *gewendon ut æt Æst geate* and got them to Eldulfsness (Walton-on-the-Naze). Mr. W. H. Stevenson, in an interesting note on personal names associated with town gates, cites an eleventh-century life of St. Edmund, in which it is called Ealsegate, and suggests that it may be named from one Ealh; the East Gate of Gloucester was called Ailesgate from Æthel.[77] A survey of Holy Trinity precinct made about 1592, and now at Hatfield, gives the plan of the gate as it then existed (possibly in part Roman), and a length of the city wall with its semicircular bastions.[78] Outside this gate the great Roman road reached away to Chelmsford and Colchester.

The principal *West Gate* is clearly Newgate, as standing opposite the East Gate and at the end of Cheap. Fabyan calls it West Gate. In the Pipe Roll for 1188 it is called Newgate, and it was then already a prison. Earlier in the twelfth century it seems to have been called Chamberlain's Gate,[79] and this name is probably explained by an entry in Domesday, where it is noted that two cottagers at Holeburn were dependent on the sheriff of Middlesex in the time of the Confessor, and that William the *Chamberlain* rendered six shillings for his vineyard [there] to the King's sheriff. That is, the Chamberlain held property outside Newgate in 1086, and the name Chamberlain's Gate probably goes back as far. An eleventh-century text of a charter dated 889[80] describes a property, "Ceolmundingehaga, not far from Westgetum." Possibly Coleman Street is named after the same citizen, who may be none other than the Ealdorman of Kent who died in 897. Outside this gate the Roman road ran west, as we have seen, to the Tyburn, beyond which it crossed the Watling Street.

Fig. 22.—From Matthew Paris, 1236.

Ludgate must have been reputed to be very ancient when Geoffrey of Monmouth wrote, early in the twelfth century. He speaks of it as "the gate which to this day is called in the British tongue Porth-Lud and in the Saxon Ludesgata." On it had been "a brazen man," said to be Cadwaladr. Dr. Rhys thinks that Geoffrey was here using ancient tradition. There is no conclusive reason why the gate should not have preserved a British name and a Roman statue, and at least the legend has a legend's worth. The next earliest mention I find of it is in the St. Paul's documents, about the middle of the twelfth century.[81] Ludgate Street without the gate is spoken of not long after. A reference cited by Fabyan, however, probably takes us back to the days of the Conquest (see below, p. 112). The Strand, leading from Westminster past St. Clement Danes to Ludgate, must be an ancient street: it may indeed represent the earliest of all paths to London from the passage of the river by the great Watling Street. St. Clement's Church, as we shall see, is pre-Conquest; Sir H. Ellis, in his introduction to Domesday, says a charter by the Conqueror refers to St. Clement Danes "in the Strand," but the actual words are not cited (vol. ii. p. 143). A street outside the western walls—"Aldwych"—is frequently mentioned from the twelfth century; it is represented by Wych Street and by Drury Lane; it turned north-west from the Strand and joined the great western highway at St. Giles, where a hospital came to be built in the Middle Ages. Lambard says Ludgate meant, in Saxon, a postern, and this meaning is found in the A.S. dictionaries. Mr. W. H. Stevenson has lately again suggested that this gate is called from a Ludd or Ludda, like Billingsgate from Billing, but on all the evidence we must conclude that the Saxon word for postern must hold the field, especially as the opposite gate in the east wall was called the Postern up to Stow's time.

Fig. 23.—The Common Seal of London, 1224.

Ealdredesgate and *Cripelegate* are both named about the year 1000 in Ethelred's Laws (Thorpe). The first is evidently called after one Ealdred. As we have seen above, in p. 79, an excavation outside Aldersgate exposed a section of the old Roman ditch, and gave evidence of a trestle bridge which crossed it from the ancient gate, which consequently must itself have been Roman.[82] Stow says that Cripplesgate is mentioned in a life of St. Edmund, which tells that the Saint's body was brought through this gate about 1010; but

85

see Aldgate above. It is named the postern of Cripplesgata in the Conqueror's charter to St. Martin's. In a slightly later charter it is called Porta Contractorum (Stow).[83] These six, with the South or Bridge Gate, make up the seven historic gates of London, and the conclusion cannot be resisted that they all date back at least to the time when Alfred repaired the walls of the city, and most, if not all of them, to Roman days. Roach Smith held that the principal gates were then Ludgate, Aldgate, and Bishopsgate. Referring to the finding of inscribed stones near to Ludgate, he says that they doubtless belonged to a cemetery which stood outside the gate. Hatton says that some Roman coins were found at Aldgate on its destruction in 1606. Price says that no evidence of the ancient wall having crossed Bishopsgate Street was found when a deep sewer was carried along the street, and hence we may infer a Roman opening in the wall at this point. Direct evidence has been found of Aldersgate, as just said, and Newgate is implied by the evidence of the Roman road found by Wren at St. Mary le Bow. FitzStephen says the city gates were double, and a rough drawing of the city in the MS. Matthew of Paris represents each gate as having two arches (Fig. 22). Stow also says that Aldgate was double. The Roman gates at Chesters and other important posts on Hadrian's Wall have coupled openings between towers containing guard chambers; the great West Gate at

Silchester was similar,[84] and we may take this gate as a type for Roman London.

We may thus form a very clear idea of what London must have looked like when the Norman Conqueror came and viewed the city walls from the other side of the river, as described by Guy of Amiens.

The assertions and contradictions in recent books, and maps founded on them,[85] are difficult to follow. According to Mr. Loftie, the north road from Bishopsgate "joined the road to Colchester and Lincoln afterwards called Erming Street" (Erming Street to Colchester); "We find both Watling and the Erming Streets going off at a tangent when they have passed out" (on plan both shown perfectly straight);[86] "Aldgate—properly Algate—was opened about the beginning of Henry's [I.] reign"; "Aldgate has nothing to do with 'Old' or Eald, for the simple reason that the eastern road ran not from Aldgate but from Bishopsgate, and not to Stratford but to Old Ford"; "Whitechapel Road—the Vicenal Way ... answered to the street of tombs without the gate at Pompeii" (in the plan a road going east from Bishopsgate is named Vicenal Way). It is impossible to say what such roads were, or where they went, or how the author knew. In the other plans mentioned above, London Bridge is shown near Billingsgate, with the north and south street *east* of St. Magnus and the north gate much to the east of Bishopsgate. Watling Street is shown on a diagonal line from

Bridge end to Newgate, and Leadenhall Street and Aldgate are omitted.

Quays.—FitzStephen, as we have seen, says that London "was walled and towered" to the south against the river. And there cannot be a doubt that the citizens were protected in this way, when we read that they shut themselves within their walls against the Danes, for land walls alone would little have availed against the water-borne hordes. Stow, Wren, and other authorities have accepted these river walls, and indeed analogy with other water-side towns calls for them. It is evident on referring to a map that Thames Street, Upper and Lower (above Bridge and below), must follow the course of this wall, and that the street was outside the wall, forming a "strand" giving access to the quays, as does the way along the Golden Horn at Constantinople. When in 1863 Thames Street was excavated, the Roman level appeared at 20 to 25 feet below the modern surface; the whole was found to have been piled and cross-timbered right across the street; this "doubtless formed the old water line and embankment fronting the south portion of Roman London." The piling turned up the course of the Walbrook towards Cannon Street.[87] Similar embankments were found when the approach to new London Bridge was made, and still further east; it is said as many as five lines were found when the present Custom House was built. Roach Smith describes the foundations of a part of the river wall which was found extending from Lambeth Hill to Queenhythe, and again by Queen Street, along the north side of the street.[88] And we have seen that the south-east and south-west angles of the wall were just on this line. Several quay basins were formed along the river shore outside the wall. The most famous of these was Billingsgate, which in the traditions of Geoffrey of Monmouth took its name from Belinus, the British Apollo. In the Laws of Ethelred (979-1015)[89] there is an item "concerning the Tolls given at Bilingesgate." It is probably the Lundentuneshythe named in a charter of 749[90] and the Roman Wharf of London.

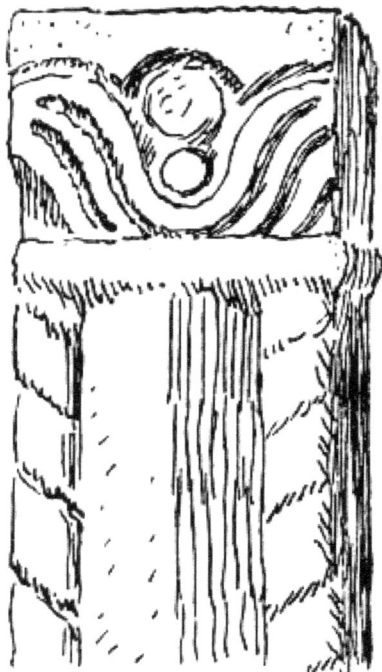

*Fig. 24.—Fragment found
in the South Wall.*

The next most important quay is Queenhythe, otherwise, as Stow says, "called Edredshithe because it at first belonged to one called Edred." This is confirmed by the name of the Church of St. Michael "Ædredeshuda" found about 1148 in the St. Paul's documents; about 1220 it appears as St. Michael's de Hutha Regina in the same. The queen who gave her name to this quay was Matilda, wife of Stephen; in the Cotton Charters (xvi. 35) is a grant from her of the hospital by the Tower and rents from Edredshythe to Holy Trinity Aldgate. In the Close Rolls of 21 Henry III. (1237) are two entries in regard to the Necessary House formerly built by Matilda, late Queen, at Queenhythe for the common use of the city; it was to be made as long as the quay of Alan Balun, so that it might have a free course of water. Dugdale cites a grant (*temp*. Henry II.) of a rent-charge on Ripa Reginæ called "Aldershithe" [?] to St. Giles. In 1247 the wharf was granted to the city at a farm of £50 a year.[91] From a charter of King Alfred himself, dated 899, we find that the Edred who gave his name to this wharf was none other than Ethered, Alfred's son-in-law and his lieutenant in London (died 912).[92] In a second version of the charter given in Birch's collection it is called Rethereshythe, but the Peterborough Chronicle again names it correctly and gives the further interesting fact that Harold held land near this quay: "*Comes Harold dedit terram in London juxta monaster. S. Pauli juxta Portum qui vocatur Etheredishithe*".[93] In a survey of the quays and approaches given in the *Liber Custumarum* a Retheresgate appears, and in a will of 1279 Retheresgate and the lane of St. Margaret near it are mentioned. The lane was later Rethers Lane and then Pudding Lane. I cannot explain the confusion as to the two sites and names. Edredshythe was walled, and the public way leading to it is mentioned. It is of great interest that its actual basin yet remains to us. If the city were not given over to all the horrors of "riches," we might hope to see a statue of the great king erected at this quay. It is of romantic interest that we can associate with this site the names of the husband of Alfred's daughter Ethelfleda, Lady of Mercia and of London, and Harold, last of the English.

Fig. 25.—Fragment found in South Wall.

Botolph's Wharf.—According to Stow, the Conqueror confirmed to Westminster Abbey "the gift which Almundus of the port of St. Botolph gave ... with the house and one wharf which is at the head of London Bridge ... as King Edward granted."

Dowgate.—In a charter of 1150-51 which Henry II. as Duke of the Normans gave to the citizens of Rouen, he grants that the men of Rouen who are free of the Merchants' Gild shall be quit of all dues save for wine and craspisce. "And the citizens of Rouen shall have at London the port of Douuegate as they have had from the time of King Edward." After warning other ships off the wharf, they were free to cut them adrift.[94] "Here then we have evidence that even before the Conquest the citizens of Rouen had a haven at the mouth of the Walbrook."[95] A chapter in the Laws of Æthelred names the traders who were free to come to the Port of London, and amongst these appear men of Flanders, France, and the Emperor's men. The men of Rouen, then, as in 1150, brought wine and craspisce (dried sturgeon or whale). From the fact that the Walbrook issued here, Dowgate has been derived from the Celtic *Dwr*, water; this would be a very interesting fact, if there were any certainty in it.

Steelyard and the Vintry Wharf.—In the privileges of the Emperor's men just mentioned we seem to have, as Dr. Sharpe suggests,[96] the beginnings of the Gilda Teutonicorum, the great mediæval Hanse by Baynard's Castle called at a late time the Steelyard. In the time of Henry II. the House of the Cologne Merchants in London is mentioned, and Richard I., when passing through Cologne, remitted the rent-charge on their Gildhall.[97] This privilege was confirmed by John in 1213.[98]

We can probably trace the port of "the Flanders men" of Æthelred's laws in a charter granted by the Conqueror to the Abbey of St. Peter's, Ghent, in 1081, granting Lewisham, Woolwich, etc.: and within London, the land which King Edward [the Confessor] gave, namely, a portion of Waremanni-Acra with the wharf belonging to it, with its market rights, stalls, shops, and dues, and that all merchants who have landed in the Soke of St. Peter [of Ghent in London] shall return and enjoy his protection. This charter is witnessed amongst others by Deorman, Leofstan, and Alward *grossus* of London.[99] In a later confirmation of 1103-09 the ground is called Wermanacre, and this name must be preserved in St. Martin's "de Beremanescherche" (date 1257);[100] for Stow says St. Martin in the Vintry was sometimes called "St. Martin de Beremund Church." Kemble gives a copy of the original charter of the Confessor, granting to St. Peter of Ghent the above-named places, also within London the land which *anglice* is called Wermanecher, with the wharf and all rights and customs. Mr. Round shows from other documents that the Confessor visited St. Peter's, Ghent, in 1016, and then promised to restore to the monks their possessions in England, and that Lewisham, etc., had first been given to the monastery as early as 918. The gift was confirmed by Edgar, with its "churches, land, and crops," at the prayer of Dunstan, who ruled St. Peter's for some time when exiled from England.

Fish hythe, in the western part of London, is named in the Saxon charter 718 of Kemble's collection. Riley, in his introduction to the *Liber Custumarum*, which contains a valuable mediæval survey of the wharves, puts Fish hythe near the bottom of Bread Street. *Ebbegate*, which is mentioned in twelfth-century documents, is, Riley says, the same as Swan Wharf.[101]

There must, even in Alfred's time, have been some sort of customs house, for there were quay dues, and a charter of 857 speaks of the place in London where the weighing and measuring of the port was done.[102]

We thus have a picture of a busy river front, the shore, backed by the city walls and gates, indented with a series of docks crowded with shipping. Says FitzStephen, "To this city from every nation under heaven merchants delight to bring their trade by sea. The Arabian sends gold, ... Gaul her wines." And Robert of Gloucester, characterising the fame of several towns, says, "London for ships most." Camden likens the docks to a floating forest.

The principal trade of the port seems to have been in slaves. A law of *c.* 685 relates to the buying of chattels in London-wic, and the traffic is frequently mentioned. Fifty years after the Conquest it was unsafe to go near the ships in Bristol harbour for fear of being kidnapped, as was young

Tristram in the story. Gildas, looking back to the commerce of the Roman period, likened the noble rivers Thames and Severn to two arms by which foreign luxuries were of old brought in. In our period a multitude of craft must have filled these basins and lined the river bank—dromonds from the Mediterranean, "long ships and round ships" from the north, and slavers from Rouen and Dublin, with many a splendid war "dragon" like Olaf Tryggvison's—"Foreward on it was a dragon's head, but afterwards a crook fashioned in the end as the tail of a dragon; but either side of the neck and all the stem were overlaid with gold. That ship the King called the Worm, because when the sail was aloft then should that be as the wings of the dragon." The ships of Cnut's English fleet were "wondrously big; he himself had that dragon which was so mickle that it told up sixty benches, and on it were heads gold bedight, but the sails were banded of blue and red and green."[103] There were also pilgrim ships, for we hear that Offa "purchased a piece of land in Flanders in order to build a house where the English pilgrims on landing might find refreshment."[104] According to the legend St. Ursula and her virgins embarked at London.

Of Alfred we are told that he built ships to fight the Danish *ashes*, "full twice as large as they, some with sixty oars, some with more." Only last year (1900) a clinker-built boat, thought to be Danish, was found on the Lea, 50 feet long and 9 feet beam. It must have been a wonderful sight when the English fleet assembled at London, as in 992, or when a great host of Northmen sailed up on the tide.

> Think that below bridge the green lapping waves
> Smite some few keels that bear Levantine staves,
> Cut from the yew wood on the burnt-up Hill,
> And pointed jars that Greek hands toiled to fill,
> And treasured scanty spice from some far sea,
> Florence gold-cloth, and Ypres napery,
> And cloth of Bruges, and hogsheads of Guienne.

CHAPTER V

THE CITADEL—SOUTHWARK—
THE DANES' QUARTER—
THE PORTLANDS AND CNIHTENGILD

Their dyke the Vikings warded,
But some deal of the war-host
Held booths in level Southwark.
Olaf the Holy in the *Heimskringla*.

The Citadel.—The Saxon Chronicle under the year 886 reads: "In this year *gesette* Alfred *Lundenburh* and gave the *burh* to Æthered the ealdorman to hold." This is usually understood to mean that Alfred restored the city wall, but Mr. John Earle in a note on the passage argues that the *burh* was a citadel. He points out that Æthelweard's Latin paraphrase reads, "*dux Æthered ... custodiendi arcem*"; he says further that *gesette* meant "founded," "peopled," and concluding that the passage means that Alfred established a military colony with an endowment of land, he suggests that we have here an account of the military occupation of Tower Hill.[105] I cannot think that the suggestion as to the limited meaning of *burh* is made out;[106] but the endowment of a garrison as suggested would give a perfect point of departure for the

"English Cnihten gild," an association to which a part of the portlands adjoining the east wall was granted, Stow says, by King Edgar. Moreover, the resumption by Alfred of London from the Danes would not only make such a body of soldiers especially necessary, but give good reason for their being called "English"; besides, it is known that Alfred did set up town garrisons. Mr. Coote has already suggested that the relinquishment in 1125 by the members of the gild of the lands which they held seems to have been in consequence of the Conqueror's garrison at his new Tower having taken over their duties. A traditional connection between the city guard and the Portsoken seems to be suggested also by the account in the *Liber Custumarum* of how the city host was wont to assemble at the west end of St. Paul's, and then march to Aldgate, where the banner of St. Paul was presented to them. The council of this force, moreover, was held in Holy Trinity, which in 1125 took over the endowment of the gild.[107]

Since writing the above I find that Mr. Oman has also argued that the Cnihten gilds of London and some other places were the military associations which Alfred and his immediate successors placed in their burhs. "That the system started with Alfred, rather than his son, seems to follow from two passages in the Anglo-Saxon Chronicle, where, under the year 894, we hear of "the King's thegns who were at home in the fortresses," and again of "the fyrd being half in the field and half at home, besides those men that held the burhs."[108]

It is likely enough that a great city like London would have had a citadel, and Tower Hill, situated at the angle of the wall by the river, seems itself to proclaim that from Roman days it has been a site of military importance. It has been doubted whether Roman buildings actually occupied the site, but some excavations in 1898-99 laid bare some remnants about three yards away from the south-west angle of the keep, together with a portion of a hypocaust.[109] Again, in the British Museum there is an ingot of silver found in the eighteenth century on the site of the Tower, and inscribed

EX OFFI

HONORII.

A similar inscribed ingot was found not long since in the *castrum* at Richborough, and this goes to raise the old theory of a treasury at the Tower again.

The account given by William of Poitiers seems to show that the Conqueror took over and added to an existing stronghold (see Freeman), and Geoffrey of Monmouth, writing within the lifetime of those who were living at the Conquest, and when the Norman Tower was barely finished, attributes the "prodigiously big tower" by Billingsgate to Belinus. Elidure, a descendant of Belinus, he tells us, was shut up in the Tower at Trinovantum (London). All tradition is in favour of its having been a stronghold before the Conquest, and Henry of Huntingdon, *c.* 1130, says that Eadric's head after his execution by Cnut was placed on the highest battlement of the Tower of London. Again, there is no tradition of the Conqueror having taken land from the city for the foundation of his Tower. "Who built the Tower of London?" asks Dr. Maitland. "Let us read what the chronicler says of the year 1097: 'Also many shires which belonged to London for work were sorely harassed by the wall that they wrought around the Tower, and by the bridge, which had been nearly washed away, and by the work of the King's Hall that was wrought at Westminster.' There were shires or districts which from of old owed work of this kind to Londonbury."[110]

According to the Welsh story, Bran the Blessed, King of Britain, "exalted from the crown of London," when wounded in battle commanded that his followers should cut off his head. "'And take you my head,' said he, 'unto the White Mount in London and bury it there with the face towards France.' And they buried the head in the White Mount. It was the third ill-fated disclosure when it was disinterred, as no invasion from across the sea came to this island while the head was in concealment." The White Hill is always explained to mean the Tower of London.[111]

101

In the story of Bran we get the constantly recurring idea of a palladium. It seems to be referred to again in Merlin's prophecy, "Till the buried kings be exposed to view in London." Some object like the statue of Pallas in Troy, and the shield of Numa in Rome, was, as it were, the soul of a city. In Geoffrey of Monmouth a brazen horse on Ludgate figures as the protecting talisman; London Stone may have had some such mystical meaning attached to it by the Saxons (see p. 181), and the Shrine of Erkenwald in St. Paul's was the sacred heart of the city in the Middle Age. That the idea of a palladium was known in Britain is proved by the case of the sacred stone of Scone—the Coronation Stone. A similar story is told of the tomb of Iver in the Saga of Ragnar Lodbrok. William the Conqueror had to break it down before he got the victory at Hastings.

Southwark or the Borough.—The Burgal Hidage, a document which has recently been critically examined,[112] containing "a list of ancient fortresses," which dates from "the days of Edward the Elder at the latest," gives us the earliest reference to Southwark. "It sets forth, so we believe, certain arrangements made early in the tenth century for the defence of Wessex against the Danish inroads. It names divers strongholds, and shows how in the great age of burh-building they had wide provinces which were appurtenant to them."

Amongst the burhs named comes Sutheringa-geweorc, in a position which is satisfied by Southwark.[113] Dr. Maitland concludes generally that the boroughs had their origin in such royal burhs founded for national defence. "The borough belongs to the genus villa (*tun*), but it was in its inception royal." The South-work was evidently a *tête-du-pont*, and became a royal borough. By means of special privileges such burhs, like the bastides of Edward I., attracted a heterogeneous population of traders, and Southwark became the great "cheaping town" of the *Heimskringla*, and "the Borough" *par excellence* to this day. In the Pipe Roll of 1130 it stands with Guildford as the second borough in Surrey, and it returned members to Parliament from the first. It must have been protected by a ditch, and remains of this, or of Cnuts dyke, might have given rise to the tradition recorded by Stow that the course of the Thames had been altered when the bridge was built by a trench cast from Rotherhithe to Battersea. The older Maitland seems to have gathered some evidence of its palisaded bank. [114] Even in the time of the Confessor the "burghers" are spoken of. Some coins of Ethelred II. bear the mint mark of Southwark: this also is a sign of being a royal burh. The whole of Surrey seems to have been under contribution for the maintenance of Southwark and Eashing [bridge?]. The churches of Southwark are of considerable antiquity. The parish church of St. Olave is mentioned 1096, and St.

George's and St. Margaret-on-the-Hill can be traced back to about 1100. Margaret Hill is the continuation of Borough High Street to St. George's Church; the name may mark a military mound.

In Domesday it appears that Southwark had been subject to the Confessor and Godwine.[115] The men of Southwark testified that in King Edward's time no one took toll on the Strand or in the Water Street save the king. Godwine had a house here, and he must have held the burh. In the dispute of 1051-52 between the Confessor and Godwine, the earl carried his forces up the river to Southwark, the burghers of which followed his cause and supported him by land. The king's navy and land force faced him from the north. The Londoners sympathised with the earl, but officially it was a case of Southwark against the city.[116]

It would probably be possible even now to lay down the course of the "walls" (of earth, like Wareham and Wallingford) by comparing the boundary of the old manor or "town" with street lines and names and other evidence. [117] Godwine's holding seems to have coincided with the gildable manor which extended along the river from St. Mary Overie's dock to Haywharf in the east, and southward nearly to St. Margaret Hill. Two other adjoining manors were included in the parliamentary area. Even the site of the great earl's manor house can, with some probability, be pointed to.[118] Excavations have shown that before Saxon days there was a considerable Roman settlement on the site of Southwark, and that the present High Street lies over the Roman approach to London. Roach Smith says that substantial remains of Roman houses have been found, particularly on both sides of the High Street up to the vicinity of St. George's Church, in which district the wall paintings and other evidence indicated villas of a superior kind. Nearer the river, where the ground had been subject to inundation, the houses were built upon piles.

In 1016 Cnut, to turn the flank of the bridge, dug a "mickle dyke" on the south, and dragged his ships to the west side of the bridge. Sir W. Besant has shown that quite a little dyke a few yards long would go round the bridge end and take a Danish ship, but he has not considered the preliminary forcing of the South-work which would have been necessary. As to the probable course of the dyke, see Allen's *History of London*, vol. i., and Faithorn's map, 1658, which shows a considerable stream flowing into St. Saviour's dock. It was required more for the investment of the stronghold than for the ships (which, as at Constantinople, could have been dragged over land), as shown by the complete passage: "They dug a great ditch on the south side, and dragged their ships to the west side of the bridge, and then afterwards ditched the city around, so that no one could go either in or out."

The Danes and their Quarter.—London Bridge was not only a roadway over the river: it was a fortification linking the walled city to the South-work and barring progress up the river. The *Knytlinga Saga* refers to this when it says: "King Cnut went with all his host to Tempsa (the Thames). In the river was built a large castle, so that a ship-host might not go up the river."

It was natural that a suburb should spring up under the shelter of the bridge along the Strand, which is probably a Roman way.

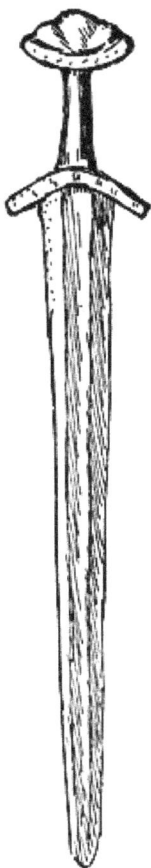

*Fig. 26.—Danish Sword
from the Thames.*

In Fabyan's Chronicle is the following curious passage referring to the reign of Ethelred: "In the third year [982] a great part of the city was wasted by fire. But you shall understand that the city of London had most building from Ludgate towards Westminster, and little or none where the heart of the city is now, except in divers places was housing, but without order, so that many cities in England passed London in building, as I have known by an old book sometime at Guildhall named Domysdaye." From another passage quoted below (p. 189) it would appear that this book was about the age of the great Domesday (1087).

FitzStephen also tells us that the Palace of Westminster was joined to the city by a *populous suburb*. In early thirteenth-century documents the Strand is sometimes called *Vico Dacorum*. The church still called St. Clement Danes certainly, as we shall see, dates from before the Conquest, and in some special way was the church of the Danes. The early existence of this western suburb would explain satisfactorily the name of Westminster, and possibly its origin. We first hear of the Abbey, independently of its own documents, towards the end of the tenth century, when in 997 Elfwic signs a charter as abbot of Westminster.[119] It is probable that Cnut was the first to choose Westminster for a royal residence, and Harold I. was buried here. All these facts go to show that the Strand in Cnut's day had become the Danish quarter. And London itself had become so Danish that Malmesbury says Harold I. was elected by the Danes and the citizens of London, who from long intercourse with these barbarians had almost entirely adopted their customs.

An account in the *Jomsvikinga Saga*, however inaccurate in detail, contains some interesting allusions to the Danes in London.

We are told that Sweyn made warfare in the land of King Ethelred and drove him out of the land; he put "*Thingamannalid*" in two places. The one in "Lundunaborg" was ruled by Eilif Thorgilsson, who had sixty ships in the "Temps," the other was north in Slesvik. The Thingamen made a law that no one should stay away a whole night. They gathered at the Bura church every night when a large bell was rung, but without weapons. He who had command in the town [London] was Eadric Streona. Ulfkel Snilling ruled over the northern part of England [East Anglia]. The power of the Thingamen was great. There was a fair there [in London] twice in every twelvemonth, one about midsummer, and the other about midwinter. The English thought it would be the easiest to slay the Thingamen while Cnut was young (he was ten winters old) and Sweyn dead. About Yule waggons went into the town to the market, and they were all tented over by the treacherous advice of Ulfkel Snilling and Ethelred's sons. Thord, a man of the Thingamannalid, went out of the town to the house of his mistress, who asked him to stay, because the death was planned of all the Thingamen by English men concealed in the waggons, when the Danes should go unarmed to the church. Thord went into the town and told it to Eilif. They heard the bell ringing, and when they came to the churchyard there was a great crowd, who attacked them. Eilif escaped with three ships and went to Denmark. Some time after, Edmund was made king. After three winters Cnut, Thorkel, and Eric went with eight hundred ships to England. Thorkel had thirty ships, and slew Ulfkel Snilling, and married Ulfhild his wife, daughter of King Ethelred. With Ulfkel was slain every man on sixty ships, and Cnut took Lundunaborg.

The massacre of the Danes at the "Bura church" must be the same event as is noticed by Stow in his account of St. Clement Danes, and also by Matthew of Westminster under the year 1012. Stow seems to suggest that it was in consequence of an attack on Chertsey Abbey. Messrs. Napier and Stevenson, in a recent reference to this story in their *Crawford Charters*, are "inclined to think that this account of the fate of the Jomsborg Thingamenn is based on real events." They have found Eilif and Thordr signing charters for Cnut. The fight with Ulfkel was at Ringmere, near Thetford.

The fact of Cnut's drawing his ships above the bridge, as described in the English Chronicles, when taken together with the above, would seem to suggest as a possibility that the intention was to reach an English fleet lying there. The Thingamannalid appears to have manned a fleet of occupation; it seems to have been none other than the original of the company of the Lithsmen of London mentioned in the

English Chronicles, and about which such various opinions have been held.[120]

Even the details of the fairs, the covered waggons, and the church-bell have some historical value. It seems probable that the Danish occupation of this quarter outside the walls of the city may date from the arrangement made between Guthrum and Alfred.

Portlands and Cnihten Gild.—London was surrounded by a wide zone of common land, the boundary of which in its late and probably lessened extent was defined by bars on the several roads, such as Temple Bar, Holborn Bar, Spital Bar, Red Cross Bar, and the bars without Aldersgate and Aldgate. These bars can be traced back to the twelfth century.[121] In 1181-88 the land or the canons of St. Paul's without the bar beyond Bishopsgate is mentioned.[122]

The "bars" seem to have been posts; those at the limit of Bridge Ward against Southwark were called "stulpes" (by Stow) or "stoples" (in 1372, Riley's *Memorials*). In the Hundred Roll of Edward I. we hear of a citizen who had put "stapellos" in front of his house.[123] From these analogies I had come to the conclusion that Staples Inn was the inn at Holborn Bars, or Staples, and I find that this suggestion has already been made because "staple" is Saxon for "post."[124] The land out to the bars is called suburbs by FitzStephen, and later, franchises or liberties. I cannot but think that the whole of this land was at times included under the designation Portsoken, which more particularly is given to that part outside the east wall of the city; thus the charter of Henry II. grants liberties "within the city and Portsoken thereof"; and the 1212 Assize of Building regulated buildings *infra Civitatem et Portsokna*. The wider liberties of the city seem to be without guarantee unless Portsoken had this extended meaning.[125]

In any case the suburbs may represent a zone of common pasture and tillage.[126] A consideration of its boundaries, however, suggests that its present form must have been governed by the growth of extra-mural population; this is also shown by the way in which extensions of boundary overlie the main roads. The Portsoken Ward must formerly have been part of this *pomærium* of the city, and it occupied most of the eastern side. Mr. Coote, in the authoritative article on the subject, calls it the city manor. The Cnihten Gild, which held it until 1125, possessed a charter of Edward the Confessor confirming to them the customs which they had in King Edgar's day.[127]

On the north side of the city the common land was called the Moor, and we have seen how a part of this "Moor" outside Cripplegate was granted to St. Martin le Grand, the rest remaining a common playground as described by FitzStephen. A mandate of Henry III. of 1268 in the Close

Rolls, however, commands the mayor and commonality "not to disturb Walter de Merton in possession of a Moor on the north side of the wall of London which the King gave to St. Paul's in consequence of the late disturbances."[128] It was fen land; FitzStephen tells how the citizens skated here, and bone skates of pre-Conquest date have been found in Moorfields. It is possible that all the common land surrounding the city was called the Fen or Moor, as a boundary on the west side against the land of Westminster was said at an early time to be in London Fen (see p. 60).[129] The 12½ acres of land, mentioned in Domesday under the name of Noman's-land, and as having been held by the Confessor, was probably some of the city land. In the fourteenth century Charterhouse was built on ground called Noman's-land—probably the same.

A part of Portsoken where fairs used to be held in the time of Henry III. was called East Smithfield; at the north-west angle of the city was another Smoothfield where the cattle fairs were held. As says FitzStephen: "Outside one of the gates immediately in the suburb is a field smooth in fact as in name. Every Friday, unless it be a feast, noble horses are here shown for sale. In another part of the field are implements of husbandry, swine, cows, great oxen, and woolly sheep.[130] On the north side there are pastures and pleasant meadow land, through which flow streams turning the wheels of mills. The tilled lands of the city are not barren soil, but fat plains producing luxuriant crops. There are also sweet springs of water which ripple over bright stones; amongst which there are Holy Well [Hoxton], Clerkenwell, and St. Clement's; they are frequented by many when they go out for fresh air on summer evenings."

It has been properly pointed out by Dr. Maitland and by Mr. Gomme that "the tilled lands of the city" is no mere rhetorical phrase,[131] but it referred to "the arable fields of the town of London." In the Saxon Chronicle we gain a sight of the citizens reaping their lands: "Then that same year [895] the Danish men who sat down in Mersey [island] towed their ships up the Thames, and thence up the Lea. This year [896] the aforesaid host wrought themselves a stronghold on the Lea, twenty miles above London. And in summer a great body of the townsmen, and other folk beside, went forth even unto this stronghold. And there were they put to flight, and there were slain some four of the king's thanes. And after, throughout harvest, did the king camp hard by the town [London] while the folk were reaping, that the Danes might not rob them of their crop. Then one day the king rode along the stream, and saw where it might be shut in, so that never might they bring out their ships. And thus was it done. And they wrought them two strongholds on the two sides of the stream. When this work was done and the camps pitched thereby, then saw the host that they might not bring out their ships. Then forsook they their ships, and fled away across the land until they came unto

Coatbridge on Severn, and there wrought they a stronghold. And the men of London took all those ships, and such as they might not bring away of them they brake up, and such as were staelwyrthe them brought they to London."

The suburbs must be the residue of the original clearing in the forest; FitzStephen says the forest was close by London and formed a covert for boars and wild cattle, and as late as the thirteenth century there were wild cattle at Osterley. [132] Scattered about the forest were village settlements, the nearest about the city mentioned in Domesday being Stepney, Hoxton, Islington, Hampstead, St. Pancras, Kensington, Chelsea. The bishop of the East Saxons already, in Alfred's day, had his house at Fulham.[133]

The citizens had their hunting rights confirmed by Henry I. "as fully as their ancestors have had, in Chiltre, Middlesex, and Surrey." Middlesex was peculiarly attached to London, and, in its modern form at least, must represent the portion of the old East Saxon kingdom cut off by Alfred's treaty with Guthrum.[134] The East Saxon kingdom, Malmesbury says, comprised the modern Essex, Middlesex, and half Hertfordshire. The Saxon Chronicle under 912 says: "This year died Æthered, and King Edward [Alfred's son] took possession of London and Oxford and of all the lands which owed obedience thereto."[135] A charter professedly dated as early as 704 names Twickenham in the province of Middlesex, but nothing is known to history of a Middle

Saxon kingdom or people. Bede says London was a city of the East Saxons, and the London bishopric is coextensive with the East Saxon kingdom, including Middlesex. If we had to find a theory for an earlier origin of Middlesex, it might be suggested that when in 571 the West Saxons and East Saxons formed their common frontiers, London with some dependent land was constituted a middle region accessible to both. This might account for the peculiar circumstances whereby London passed successively under the suzerainty of one state after another. Middlesex was in fact the "country of London," as it is called by Capgrave.

Besides the suburban land, there remained much common and open land in the city itself through the Middle Ages.[136] Stocks Market, for instance, "the middle of the city," as Stow says, was made in 1282 on "an open space where, the way being very large and broad, had stood a pair of stocks." This looks like the "village green" of London. In the original grant in the *Liber Custumarum* the vacant land is described as north of Woolchurch, where the king's beam stood and the wool market was held.

At the east end, near the precinct of the Tower, some ground bore the name of Romeland, whatever that may mean:[137] at the west of the city was St. Paul's Churchyard, with the areas where the folkmote met, and where the city host assembled in arms.

It was not till the centuries following the Conquest that the ground just within the walls seems to have been appropriated; at least large sections remained to be occupied by the monasteries of Holy Trinity, St. Helen's, Austin Friars, and Greyfriars. The orchards and gardens of citizens are frequently mentioned. A deed of 1316 refers to a grant of land called Andovrefield and a house called Stonehouse by the Walbrook.[138] London in Saxon times indeed was a walled county, and up to the sixteenth century retained much of its character as a "garden city."

The Cnihtengild, which till 1125 held the Portsoken, has been incidentally dealt with in the course of this chapter (pp. 102 and 118). Of the many problems connected with the history of London, hardly one has been more discussed than the status of this "mysterious institution." Mr. Loftie thought he had proved that the aldermen formed its members, and that it was the governing gild of London. Mr. Round, however, has adversely criticised this conclusion. It is certain that there were Cnihtengilds in other places, as Winchester and Exeter. As all such places appear to have been county strongholds or burhs, and as we have seen it is probable that the Cnihts of London had the duty of defending the city, and further, as at Cambridge the members of a gild of Thegns were called Cnihts, I conclude the members of the London gild were originally the Thegns who garrisoned Londonburh.[139]

CHAPTER VI

THE WARDS AND PARISHES—THE PALACE

So Hawk fared west to England to see King Athelstane, and found the king in London, and thereat was there a bidding and a feast full worthy. So they went into the hall thirty men in company, and Hawk went before the king and greeted him, and the king bade him welcome.

Saga of Harold Hairfair.

Wards and Parishes.—The earliest lists of wards which give the present traditional names have been printed by Dr. Sharpe in his *Calendar of London Wills* and his *Letter Book A.* These are of about the years 1320, 1293, and 1285. Another of 1303 is in Palgrave's *Treasury.* A patent of 1299 speaks of the mayor and twenty-four aldermen. Before this time most of the wards were called by the names of the aldermen holding them, as said in the *Liber Albus.* There is a list of this kind, in which only a few of the traditional names appear, in the Hundred Rolls of 1275. This last is particularly interesting, however, as giving the names of the city magnates of the great time just after the war of the city with the king, when Thomas FitzThomas, the mayor, was imprisoned—some have said never to appear again; but I find in the Close Rolls for 1269-70 (53 Henry III.) that in that year "Thomas son of Thomas, late Mayor of London," entered into recognisances for a debt of £500 to Edward the king's son, finding sureties for the same and for his fealty to the king and his heirs.

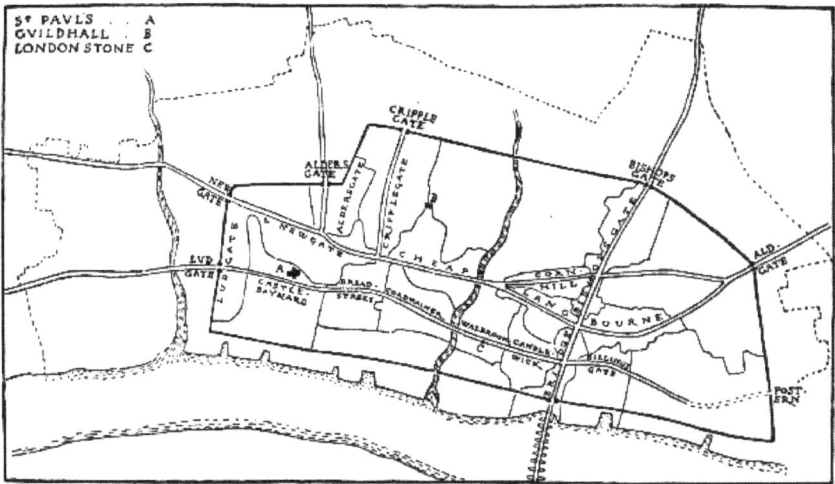

Fig. 27.—Plan showing the relation of the central Wards and the principal Streets

Another list of aldermen in 1214 is printed in Madox's *Exchequer*, together with a reference to one of 1211, which carries back the complete list of twenty-four to within twenty years of the institution of the mayoralty.

An account of the property of St. Paul's made in the first half of the twelfth century, and printed in facsimile in Price's *History of the Guildhall*, incidentally contains a list of about twenty wards, mostly under the names of their aldermen. Of these "*Warda Fori*" and the wards of Aldgate, Brocesgange (Walbrook), and of the Bishop may be cited as especially interesting; Aldresmanesberi is also mentioned. This document is not dated, but Mr. Round has shown it to have been written about 1130. Hugo, son of Wlgar, and Osbert, Aldermen, occur in another deed of 1115, and Thurstan, Alderman, in 1111. Mr. Loftie has attempted to identify some of the wards. The Ward of Herbert, in which was the land of William Pontearch, may perhaps be Dowgate, for a charter of Stephen gave to S. M. de Sudwerc the stone house of William de Pontearch, situated by the sheds of Douegate (Dugdale). What is probably a still earlier group of aldermen is given in a Ramsay document of 1114-30, which is addressed to Hugo de Bochland, Roger, Leofstan, Ordgar, and all the other barons (*i.e.* aldermen) of London. Another document of the same age is witnessed by Levenoth, "Alderman." A careful comparison of these lists, together with other sources,[140] might yield some new facts. From a cursory comparison it seems to be evident that too much has been made of the case of the Farndons and Farringdon Ward as evidence for hereditary *ownership* in the aldermanries. Most of the family names change from list to list, but a few persist: in 1240 there is a Jacob Bland, in 1275-85 and 1293 a Rudulphus Blond, but this may be the case in any office. On the other hand, two of the same family name are found more than once holding different wards at the same time, and in other cases similar names are found in different wards in different lists; thus in 1285 there are two Ashys, two Rokesleys, two Boxes, and two Hadstocks: a Frowick in 1285 held Cripplegate, and in 1320 a Frowick held Langbourne. The ward that can most easily be traced is Cheap; in 1211-14 it was held by William son of Benedict, in 1275 by Peter of Edmonton, in 1285 by Stephen Ashy, and in 1320 by Simon Paris. This is hardly hereditary succession. But what I am concerned with is not the tenure but the topographical origin of the wards. Many different theories as to the origin of the wards have been put forward. Mr. Loftie, writing of the beginning of the thirteenth century, says: "The wards, as we shall notice more distinctly further on" (the distinctness is difficult to find), "were in the hands originally of the landowners, and an alderman was still very much in the position of a lord of the manor. His office was at first always, and still usually, hereditary." After the reign of Henry III. the aldermen no longer owned their wards. The constitution had undergone a complete change, "and the offices became purely elective."

Mr. Price thought that the wards were divisions dating from Roman days. Norton believed that the wards were to the city what the hundreds were to the shire, and this view, shared by Bishop Stubbs, seems to be confirmed, as will be shown by an independent line of reasoning.

The wards can be traced back to within fifty years after the Conquest, and that they were even then of immemorial antiquity is shown by FitzStephen's legend that, like Rome, London was founded by the Trojans, and consequently had the same laws, and like it was divided into wards. In Cambridge there were ten wards in 1086.

A study of the ward boundaries in connection with the Walbrook, the "Carrefour," and the main streets yields most interesting results. Stow tells us that a great division between the western and eastern wards was made by the Walbrook, which ran from the north wall to St. Margaret's Lothbury, then under Grocers' Hall, and St. Mildred's Church, west of the Stocks Market, through Bucklersbury, then by the west of St. John's Walbrook and the Chandlers' Hall, and by Elbow Lane to the Thames. On laying down the course of this stream from all obtainable data, it is found that it was an unbroken boundary between the thirteen eastern and eleven western wards.

Again, the four principal cross streets form so many backbones to a series of wards; and this in such a marked way as to show on a good map quite certainly at a glance, that these wards were formed by aggregations of dwellings upon either side of the roads which passed through them, exactly as a high-road threads a village.

Bridge Ward is a narrow strip containing the Bridge Street up to the cross of Lombard Street. Bishopsgate

Ward, beginning at this same crossways, goes all the way to Bishopsgate, the ward street passing through its midst.

Lombard Street and Fenchurch Street furnish the midrib to Langbourne Ward[141] in just as obvious a way. Stow thought that Langbourne Ward was called from a stream, but this has been shown to be untenable for physical reasons (see p. 48); and the plan of the wards shows instantly that here was no water-course, like the Walbrook, *dividing* wards, but a street passing through the *midst* of a ward. While deriving this *ward's* name from a brook, Stow says that Lombard *Street* was so called of the Longobard merchants about 1300. I find that the *street* was called Langbourne Strate at the end of the thirteenth century;[142] and in a charter of Matilda to Holy Trinity, 1108-18, appears the Church of St. Edmund in *Longboard Strete*. The first mention I can find of the ward is also of the twelfth century; this is a demise by "Geoffrey, Alderman of the Ward of Langebord," of land in Lime Street. [143] It is evident from this that the name of the street and the ward was originally one and the same—Langbard, Longbord, or Longford, as it occasionally appears. The street was written "Lumbard Strete" in 1319.[144]

The St. Paul's documents show that important Lombards were resident in London early in the twelfth century, and they probably gave their name to the ward and street; two of these were Meinbod and his son Picot the Lombard. In Paris there is a Lombard Street, and other cities have the name. And the word is written Langeberde in old English.

Cornhill Ward, Cheap Ward, and the old Newgate Ward are just as clearly three wards strung on the street which respectively threads them in passing to the west gate, and properly takes the name of each ward in passing through it.

Lime Street and Aldgate Wards lie over Leadenhall (the old Aldgate) Street; from the look of it we might suppose that Lime Street Ward was formerly part of Aldgate Ward, as the *division* line is here formed by the street which gives its name to the ward. The backbone of Tower Ward is Great Tower Street, which passes into Billingsgate Street as East Cheap, and on westward as Candlewick Street. Coleman Street threads the ward of the same name, which is possibly derived from the Coleman named on p. 83, and Cripplegate and Aldersgate Wards are formed on the ancient streets which went to those gates.

This examination of the forms of the wards in relation to the ancient streets which they overlie is enough to prove irresistibly that the main streets of the city existed before the wards, and that these wards originated not as "private property," but as units of population inhabiting the houses along those streets, like so many villages or townships. These streets, in turn, however long and unbroken, evidently bore different names according to the wards they passed through.

The study of the wards might be carried further in one direction by means of a map on which the boundaries of the parishes, as well as of the wards, were carefully laid down. Although upwards of a hundred parishes can hardly date back so early as the institution of wards, it is possible that certain large parishes may have had an origin identical with the wards,[145] and most of them probably date from before the Conquest. It would be interesting also to compare the boundaries of the suburban parishes with the limits of the suburbs proper as defined by the bars.

It is generally accepted that a parallel holds between the organisation of the city and the shire, the ward and the hundred. "Hundreds and Tithings were part of the primitive Germanic constitution." Dr. Stubbs has shown that in Domesday several towns figure as hundreds, and the wards of the city of Canterbury were called hundreds. Thus too, I suppose, it arose that the reports of the wards of London were inserted in the Hundred Rolls.

The wards in London most probably represented the groups of citizens belonging to several gilds; they may indeed be identical with the Peace gilds of Athelstane's enactment, according to which the population were to be enrolled by tens and hundreds in associations for the preservation of peace and the suppression of theft.[146] In accordance with this idea of accounting for every man, we find that even in the thirteenth century no one was to stay in the city for more than two nights "unless he finds two sureties and so puts himself in frankpledge." The aldermen were responsible for their wards,[147] and every hosteller was likewise responsible for his guest.[148] Dr. Maitland suggests that the Aldermen were the military captains of the burgmen. It is certain that the defence of the town gates was assigned to the men of the several wards.

The wards, then, were in the main organisations for the executive government, the ordering and policing of the city. "The ward-mote is so called as being the meeting together of all the inhabitants of a ward in presence of its head, the alderman, or else his deputy, for the correction of defaults, the removal of nuisances, and the promotion of the well-being of each ward."[149] This function, indeed, is explained by the very name "ward," and the "frankpledge" was a survival of primitive adoption into the tribe. Some recognition of this is made by Holinshed, who says the city is divided into twenty-six wards or "tribes." It even seems possible that the wards may at first have been formed by symmetrical numerical units such as, say, a hundred freemen; or the space within the walls may have been divided up into twenty or twenty-four parts in such a way as to allow for density of population. Excavations in the city have shown that the population clustered most thickly along the river and in the great streets, and the wards are much more congested and regular in the central part by the bridge than nearer the walls: the old churches also seem to gravitate towards the same nucleus.

Wards without.—A good illustration of the formation of the interior wards may be found in the growth of those without the walls. Bishopsgate Without, and Aldersgate Without, were evidently formed by clusters of dwellings springing up on either side of the roads outside the gates. Cottages outside Bishopsgate and at Holborn are mentioned even in Domesday, and Fleet Street appears to have been populous even earlier. The external wards extend to the boundary of the city liberties, or common land, and the roads passing through them had specific street-names as far as the several "Bars." Holborn Street, as it is sometimes called, which passed over the Hole-burn, should properly end with the city liberty, as does Fleet Street.

Along with the wards were a number of sokes—areas in which persons or corporations held certain privileges. The first sokes mentioned are that of the Cnihten Gild (pre-Conquest), and that of St. Peter of Ghent (in 1081, see p. 97). The charter of Henry I. grants that "no guest tarrying in any soc shall pay custom to any other than him to whom the soc belongs." They appear to have been heritable, and free to some extent from civic jurisdiction: in the reign of Edward I. there were still upwards of twenty in existence in

London.[150] "Bury" seems to have been applied to a manor or property surrounded by a wall or fence; "in London," says Mr. W. H. Stevenson, "it means a large house." Bucklersbury and Bloomsbury were the properties—post-Conquest—of one Blemund, and of the family of Bockerel. A Saxon will makes a bequest to Paul's byrig.[151] The termination "haw," present still in Bassishaw, is also common. A charter of the Confessor giving Stæninghaga in London to Westminster is printed by Kemble; Dr. Maitland in *Domesday and Beyond* has shown that this was occupied by the men of Staines, and that Staining Lane probably preserves its memory even unto this day. There were forty-eight burgesses of London who counted with Staines in 1086. He suggests that we have here a trace of a system by which the shires garrisoned the burhs.

The Palace.—There are but few references to a palace. Florence, writing of 1017, says that Cnut "being in London" ordered Edric to be "slain in the palace" and his body to be thrown from the walls—"into the Thames," says Malmesbury. Richard of Cirencester, who wrote in the middle of the fourteenth century, but whose testimony is of the more value as he was a monk at Westminster, says that Cnut was keeping his Christmas "in the castle which is now called Baynard's," and after the death of Edric took boat for

Westminster. There is every reason to think that the ruler's house in London, as in Constantinople, Venice, Aachen, and Paris, would have adjoined the cathedral, as Baynard's Castle did. That Baynard's Castle should have been the old royal palace would seem to agree very well with its subsequent history; it would also explain the existence of this stronghold held under the king within the city walls, while none of the chroniclers speak of its site being taken from the city, and it would explain why early in the twelfth century Henry I. should give a part of the site to St. Paul's; for, if it had been built after the Conquest, it would hardly have been curtailed so early.[152]

Henry of Huntingdon says that William Baynard was deprived of his estate in 1110. It was then, I suppose, that it passed to the Clares. The Fitzwalters, who held it after Baynard, belonged to the great family of the Clares.[153] Baynard's Castle was probably dismantled under John when the king quarrelled with Fitzwalter. In 1275 a patent was granted R. Fitzwalter to alienate Castle Baynard near the city walls, with stone wall, void areas, ditches, and even the tower of Fish Street Hill. Taking this and the St. Paul's document together, the precinct seems to have included the ground between the boundary of St. Paul's (along Carter Lane) and the river and from the city wall to Old Fish Street. It must have been an important castle, not a mere tower.

Henry II. is made by Fantosme to ask how "mes baruns de Lundres ma cité" fared in the troubles of that time, and is told that Gilbert de Munfichet had strengthened his "castle," and that the Clares were leagued with him. This Montfichet's Castle is mentioned by FitzStephen, and Stow says that it was close to Castle Baynard towards the west, and on the river; but a document given by Dugdale speaks of Munfichet Castle with its ditch as close to Ludgate (ii. 384).[154]

Tradition has also assigned the site of a Saxon palace close to the east end of St. Alban's, Wood Street. It was said that King Athelstane had his house here, which, having a door into Adel Street, "gave name to this street, which in ancient evidences is written King Adel Street."[155] Stow just refers to the story, but says any evidence had been destroyed, and he was evidently disgusted at a then recent "improvement." Some accounts of 23 Henry VIII., given in the *Calendar of St. Paul's Documents*, refer to the "clensying of certyn old ruinouse houses in Aldermanbury, sometime the palace of Saincte Æthelbert Kyng ... and making of five new tenements." It is curious that there is an Adle Hill, also in Castle Baynard Ward. The records of St. Alban's show that Abbot Paul (from 1077) obtained by exchange with the Abbot of Westminster what was said had been the chapel of Offa's palace near the church of St. Alban's, Wood Street. This evidently refers to the same site abutting on St. Alban's, Wood Street.[156] It has been said that Gutter Lane is named from the residence of Guthrum. I find it called Godron Lane in early documents, and the tradition may possibly be true (see p. 154).

Tower Royal was a royal residence after the Conquest; Stow says Stephen lodged there.[157] Froissart, writing of the Wat Tyler's rebellion, tells how the king's mother fled to "the Royal called the Queen's Wardrobe."

We get in the *Heimskringla* a fair picture of what the king's haga or garth would have been in the history of King Olaf the Holy. "King Olaf let house a king's garth at Nidoyce. There was done a big court hall with a door at either end, but the high seat of the king was in the midmost of the hall. Up from him sat his court-bishop, and next to him again other clerks of his; but down from the king sat his counsellors. In the other high seat strait over against him sat his marshal, and then the guests. By litten fires should ale be drunk. He had about him sixty body-guards and thirty guests. Withall he had thirty house carles to work all needful service in the garth. In the garth also was a mickle hall wherein slept the body-guard, and there was withal a mickle chamber where the king held his court chambers." Of Olaf the Quiet we are told: "That was the ancient wont in Norway that the king's high seat was midst of the long daïs, and ale was borne over the fire. But King Olaf was the first let do his high seat on the high daïs athwart the hall.... He let stand before his board trencher-swains. He had also candle-swains, who held

131

up candles before his board. Out away from the trapeza was the marshal's stool."

CHAPTER VII

STREETS—CRAFT GILDS AND SCHOOLS—CHURCHES

They answered and said that there were many more churches there [in London] than they might wot to what man they were hallowed.

Heimskringla.

Streets.—As has been said, a large number, probably most, of the streets of London as they existed before the fire can be traced in records back to the thirteenth century. It is evident that the extra-mural approaches and the gates necessitated the existence of some of these at a still earlier time; the sites of ancient churches and the formation of the wards to which the streets serve as midribs, as above said, account for others. That some are of Roman date positive evidence has been found. On reviewing this cumulative evidence it seems possible that the main streets given in Stow's *Survey* represent ways in the Roman city. A succession of fires slowly raising the surface with layers of debris, gradual encroachments, and the obliteration of open spaces, have modified the old lines in some cases considerably, but still it is certain, I believe, that the general "squareness" and more or less symmetrical alignment of the Roman city can be traced in the existing streets. A line from the bridge to the north gate must always have formed a great main street, and standing at the bottom of Bridge Street (Fish Street Hill) we may still gain some idea of what the entrance to the city by the Roman bridge was like. Mr. Price says of Gracechurch Street: "Recent investigations have shown ... that no structural remains of the Roman period can have occurred throughout its course; on either side of the street, debris of buildings with fragments of tessellated pavements have been seen, but nothing has existed along the actual line of road."[158] Roach Smith also testifies that no wall has been found crossing Gracechurch Street, "a fact that would support the opinion of its occupying the route of one of the Roman roads."[159] The idea of J. R. Green, that the north and south street was considerably to the east of the present line, was probably founded on Stow's mistaken view that the bridge was of old far to the east.

Again, for the two great longitudinal ways through the city we have evidence. In forming the entrance into the city from New London Bridge a section was made of the ground north of Thames Street, and three ancient lines of embankment were found, by which ground was by degrees regained from the Thames. One of these was formed of squared oaks. As the excavation came to Eastcheap it crossed a raised bank of gravel 6 feet deep and 18 wide, the crest of which was 5 feet under the present surface; it ran in the direction of London Stone. On reaching the north-east corner of Eastcheap the foundations of a Roman building were found, and here, having reached the line of Gracechurch Street, the discoveries ended.[160] Roach Smith speaks of walls having been found in Eastcheap and Little Eastcheap, but Cannon Street, like Gracechurch Street, was free from them.

It has been conjectured that Cheapside was not a street, that it was a muddy marsh, an open space for market booths, and that a stream ran from it into Walbrook, etc.[161] Two deeds, however, given in Dugdale under Barnstaple, record the gift of a new house and land in "*Foro*" or "*Magno Vico Londoniæ quam habuit Odone Bajocensi*" by William Gifford, Bishop of Winchester, to S. Martin Paris, 1110-15, and this reference to the property of Odo of Bayeux carries Cheapside right back to Conquest days. It is not unlikely, indeed, that the east end of the "Great Street" was the site of the Roman Forum or part of it. The "Forum" of Canterbury is mentioned in 762.[162] Although the word Forum doubtless stands only for the Saxon market-place, it was the proper place of assembly. According to the *Acta Stephani* the Empress Maud was acclaimed Lady of England in the Forum of Winchester. There is no doubt Cheap was the Saxon High Street and the official meeting-place of the citizens from the earliest days of the English settlement. Early in the twelfth century Thomas à Becket was born in his father's house in Cheap, on a site we can still identify, and Eudo, Dapifer to the Conqueror, also appears to have had a stone house in West Cheap, by Newchurch.

When Wren rebuilt St. Mary le Bow, in excavating for the foundation of the campanile, when he had sunk about 18 feet, he came to a Roman causeway of rough stone, close and well rammed, with Roman brick and rubbish for a foundation, all firmly cemented. This causeway was 4 feet thick, and underneath was the natural clay. He built the tower "upon the very Roman causeway." He was of the opinion that this highway ran along the north boundary of the Roman city, the breadth of which was from this "causeway" to the Thames, and "the principal middle street or Prætorian way" being Watling Street; north of the "causeway" the ground was a morass, so that he had to pile for building the new east front to St. Lawrence by the Guildhall.[163] Too much has been made of this morass, for remains of Roman buildings have been found on this very ground north of Cheap 17 feet below the surface,[164] and St. Lawrence itself had been a church from Norman times at least. Other Roman buildings have been found in Wood Street.[165]

It is impossible to go behind Wren's testimony as to the Roman way through Cheap. It has been claimed, however, that some foundations discovered by him on the site of St. Paul's showed that Watling Street ran obliquely from London Stone to Newgate. It was not, as we see, the opinion of Wren himself, and it must fall. The exact words in *Parentalia* cited for the discovery of an oblique street are themselves enough to abolish the theory built on them. They are as follows: "Upon demolishing the ruins [of St. Paul's] and searching the foundations of the Quire, the Surveyor [Wren] discovered nine wells in a row, which no doubt had anciently belonged to a street of houses that lay aslope from the High Street [Watling Street] to the Roman causeway [Cheapside], and this street, which was taken away to make room for the new Quire [of 1256] came so near to the old [Norman] Presbyterium that the church could not extend farther that way at first" (p. 272). There is nothing in this about "a Watling Street running from Newgate to London Stone." What is described is a way across the churchyard from the west end of the High or Atheling Street issuing by Canon Row or Ivy Lane. There is no evidence at all, then, for a diagonal Watling Street which Stukeley suggested, and more recent writers have accepted as quite proven. On the other hand, we have Wren's great authority for thinking that Watling Street was in its present direction the "High Street" of the ancient city. In calling it this he must have followed Leland, who says that it was formerly called Ætheling Street, and it is so named in thirteenth-century documents.[166] In 1212 I find *ad viam que vocatur* Athelingestrate. The name is one of a class of which Athelney (Athelingey—Noble's Island) is an instance. Addle Hill, which Stow calls Adle Street, seems to be allied to Atheling. In 1334 I find "Athele

Street in Castle Baynard Ward."[167] The earliest instance of "Watling" I can find is at least a century later. I am speaking, of course, of the city street; for the great Watling Street we have evidence which goes up to the eighth century (see p. 54).

There cannot be a doubt that the Roman street system was carried on by the Saxons; at Rochester as early as the seventh century Southgate Street and Eastgate Street are named in a charter. A charter of Alfred's time (889) mentions a court and ancient stone edifice in London, called by the citizens Hwætmundes Stone, between the *public street* and the wall of the city. A property in London between Tiddberti Street and Savin Street (? Seething Lane) is mentioned as a gift of Ethelbald's.[168] The Watmund's Stone named above may have been a house. A curious piece of topographical embroidery has been wrought round about it, for no less an authority than Mr. John Earle accepted the suggestion that the name might be equivalent to Corn-basket, and that the monument now in Panyer Alley may represent the ancient "stone edifice"! Mr. Round, in relation to this, has pointed out that Watmund was merely a commonly used man's name. Mr. Loftie, however, boldly says that Alfred's corn market stood to the west of Cheap, "where there was a weighing stone for wheat."[169]

Fig. 28.—Saxon Brooch found in Cheapside.

The crossing of the great streets at Leadenhall Market was called the "Carfukes of Leadenhall" in 1357.[170] This four-ways was probably marked by a market cross like the Carfax at Oxford. At Exeter there was a Carfax,[171] and there was also one at Paris.[172] It is thus that Leadenhall Market sprang up at the main crossing of the city. At this centre the continuous routes change their names after the model of the usual north-, south-, east-, and west-gate streets of other towns: (1) Bishopsgate Street; (2) Gracechurch

Street and Bridge Street; (3) Aldgate Street (now Leadenhall); (4) Cornhill, Cheap, and Newgate Street. The secondary crossing at Lombard Street, Stow calls the "Four ways." At the meeting of Cheap, Cornhill, and Lombard Street was the Stocks Market, which Stow says was the centre of the city; here stood the stocks and pillory. The names Cheap, and Cornhill or "Up-Cornhill," can be traced back to about 1100. Several other streets are named in documents of the twelfth century, as Milk Street and Broad Street (1181), Fridaie Street, Mukenwelle or Muchwella (Monkwell) Street, Candelwrich (Cannon) Street, Godrun Lane, East Cheap, The Jewry, Alsies (Ivy) Lane, Vico Piscaro (1130), Lombard Street, and Lime Street. This early occurrence of Godrun's Lane goes to confirm the tradition that it was named from the Danish leader: there is still a Guthrum's Gate at York. Alsie was the name of the Portreeve to whom the Confessor addressed a charter: it is interesting that Ivy Lane (it is Dr. Sharpe's identification) may commemorate his name to this day. Each principal street was a "King's Street" or *Via Regia*, as in the laws of Ethelred. The laws of Athelstane provide that "all marketing be within the port (town) and witnessed by the Portreve or other unlying man." That is in "open market."

Fig. 29.—Coin of Alfred with
Monogram of London. Enlarged.

From the moment when we first hear of it London
has been a famous port and market. Tacitus speaks of it as
"celebrated for the resort of merchants with their stores."
"London," says Beda, speaking of the opening of the seventh
century, "was a mart town of many nations which repaired
hither by sea and land."

In Athelstane's appointment of moneyers to the realm
London was assigned eight, this being two more than any

other place. The coins of Alfred struck in the city form a large series. The monogram of London which fills the reverse of some of them is a quite perfect design,[173] and it deserves to be better known and largely used (Fig. 29).

As to the relation of Saxon and Roman London a few words may be said. Wren held that the Roman Forum was at London Stone, while Stukeley suggested the Stock's Market on the site of the present Exchange. Excavations at Chesters and Silchester have shown that the forum in each case occupied a large "insula" right in the centre of the city, and this would agree best with Stukeley's site. [174] It is possible that it may have extended along by the east bank of the Walbrook as far as Cannon Street. The assumption of old writers, that Roman London would be symmetrically planned, with streets crossing at right angles, is not necessarily true. The streets of mediæval London in their main lines were not more irregularly laid out than the streets of Pompeii. The recently excavated city of Silchester is more regular, but this city was probably laid out once for all, whereas London was just as probably the result of gradual growth. In many respects, however, Silchester affords a close parallel to London.

In the *Conquest of England* Mr. Green stated the view that Saxon London "grew up on ground from which the Roman city had practically disappeared." He inferred this "from the change in the main line of communication" from Newgate to the bridge. According to Mr. Loftie's last word, given in the Memorial volume of 1899, the London recovered by Alfred was a ruined wall enclosing nothing. The bridge stood much farther down stream than now. To protect it the king built a tower at the south-east corner of the walls. The Roman streets did not exist or were useless. He (why he?) made a road diagonally from the bridge to Westgate. The old Bishopsgate was to the east of the present one, and opened on the road to Essex, etc. My view of Alfred's London is that the Roman city to a large degree continued to exist, and the streets were still maintained, by the new population. Here a Roman mansion with its mosaic floors would still be inhabited. There a portico would be patched with gathered bricks and covered with shingles, while by its side stood a house of wattle and daub. Here was a Roman basilican church, while in another place would be found one of timber and thatch. When a church is distinguished by being called a stone church (like St. Magnus), it is evident that others were less substantial. Garden and tillage filled up wide interspaces. In the Assise of Buildings of 1212 it is said that "in ancient times the greater part of the city was built of wood, and the houses were covered with straw and stubble and the like." Daubers and mudwallers were much in request right through the Middle Age.[175]

Roach Smith, who had an expert's knowledge of all the data in regard to Roman London, held that the approach was along High Street, Southwark, that the bridge was on the site of that destroyed about 1830, that Bishopsgate represented one of the chief gates, Aldgate and Ludgate being others, and that the crossing of East Cheap with Gracechurch Street was probably the centre of an earlier and smaller city. Quantities of Roman bricks, he says, have been found re-used in the walls of early houses and churches, and obviously taken from Roman buildings which occupied their sites. It is probable indeed that some Roman buildings were still in use in the Middle Age—for instance, the so-called Chamber of Diana near St. Paul's, and "Belliney's Palace" at Billingsgate.

Craft Gilds and Schools.—As far back as we have any body of record to go upon we find that important men in the city were craftsmen—goldsmiths, weavers, dyers, tailors, cobblers, tanners. They held offices and owned land, and the only other class at once large numerically and important in position seems to have been the clergy. Early in the twelfth century the St. Paul's documents twice at least make use of the style "mercator," and still earlier in Anglo-Saxon laws we have Ceipman.

There is every probability that the craft gilds date from before the Conquest. In the twelfth century head masons, carpenters, and other craftsmen are called "masters," and this title of university rank was always, I believe, formally conferred by an organised gild. Even at this time the members of crafts were grouped together, as witness Candlewright Street, Milk Street, and the Shambles. We hear of a weaver's gild in 1130.[176] Even before the Conquest, probably, craftsmen wrought and sold their ordinary wares in the traditional open-fronted shops known as well in the East as in mediæval Europe.

FitzStephen says there were three principal schools in London when he wrote (in the twelfth century). St. Paul's School, almost certainly, was already established at the Conquest, and the schools of *S. Marie Archa* and *S. Martini Magni* are mentioned in a mandate about 1135 (*Commune of London*, p. 117).

Churches.—So many churches can now be traced back to the twelfth century that there cannot be a doubt that FitzStephen was accurate in saying that at that time there were in London and the suburbs thirteen larger conventual churches, besides lesser parish churches one hundred and twenty-six. In other words, practically all the parish churches in London and its liberties had been founded by the end of the twelfth century; and there is every reason for supposing that many, if not most, of these churches were even then ancient.

St. Paul's.—The cathedral we know from Bede was founded early in the seventh century by Mellitus, sent from Rome in 601 and consecrated Bishop of London by St. Augustine in 604.

The fourth bishop in succession to the "Mellifluous Mellitus" was Erkenwald, "Light of London," *Christi lampas Aurea* (675-693). It is said that he was son of Offa, the East Saxon king, who remained "paynim," but Erkenwald "changed his earthly heritage for to have his heritage in heaven; ... and whatsomever he taught in word he fulfilled in deed." He founded the monasteries of Barking and Chertsey. While he was bishop he used to preach about the city from a cart, and once, when a wheel fell off, the cart went forward without falling, "which was against reason and a fair miracle." He died at Barking, and the monks claimed his body, but "a chapter of Paul's and the people" said it should be brought to London. As they carried him to his own church there was a flood, but the waters of the Yla (Lea) were divided and a dry path given to the people of London, "and so they came to Stratford and set down the bier in a fair mede full of flowers, and anon after the weather began to wax fair and the people were full of joy." And, after, they laid and buried the body in St. Paul's, to the which he hath been a special protection against fire, nd time was when he was seen in the church with a banner fighting a fire which threatened to burn the whole city, and so saved and kept his church.[177]

The shrine of Erkenwald remained from this time till the Reformation the palladium of the city.

Fig. 30.—Tomb of King Ethelred in Old St. Paul's.

In Saxon charters the church is styled "St. Paules mynstre on Lundene," and the full invocation appears to have been *Beati Pauli Apostoli Gentium Doctoris*, which in itself probably explains the choice of it for a mission church. Like the church which Augustine built at Canterbury, it would have been "planned in imitation of the Great Basilica of Blessed Peter." Such a basilica of considerable size is still to be seen at Brixworth, Northamptonshire. It would have had a narthex, a nave with "porticoes" or aisles, and beyond the great arch a presbytery and apse. In front would have been an atrium.[178]

Under 961 the Saxon Chronicle says: "And St. Paul's minster was burnt and in the same year again founded." King Ethelred was buried in St. Paul's in 1016, and his tomb, a fine stone chest, stood here till the great fire of London. There is no reason why the tomb illustrated by Dugdale should not be the original one of 1016 (Fig. 30). Next to it was the similar tomb of Sebba, king of the East Saxons, who was buried at the end of the seventh century. The only material memorial of the Saxon minster now existing is a tombstone inscribed in runes, "Kina let this stone be set to Tuki." It was found in 1852 in the south churchyard, 20 feet below the surface, in an upright position, forming the headstone of a grave composed of stone slabs. The bottom portion was irregular and untooled; this, which showed that it was a headstone, was cut off to make it a tidy antiquity, but it is otherwise carefully preserved in the Guildhall Museum, and bears a sculpture of a fine knotted dragon.

*Fig. 31.—Ninth or Tenth Century Tombstone
from St. Paul's Churchyard.*

Wren, who was a critical observer of the evidence which
came to light when preparing the ground for the new church,
gave but little credit to the story that a temple of Diana once
stood on the site. "But that the north side of this ground had
been very anciently a great burying-place was manifest, for
in digging the foundations of St. Paul's he found under the
graves of later ages, in a row below them, the burial-places of
Saxon times—some in graves lined with chalk stones, some
in coffins of whole stones. Below these were British graves.

In the same row but deeper were Roman urns—this was 18 feet deep or more." Wren thought that the Prætorian camp had been here in Roman days.[179]

St. Peter's-upon-Cornhill claims to be the oldest church in London, and to have been the stool or a Romano-British archbishop. The pretension seems to have been recognised by St. Paul's in the Middle Ages, and Bishop Stubbs was inclined to accept the archbishopric as having existed in London. As the interval in Church continuity cannot have been long, it is most likely that Mellitus reconsecrated some Roman temples or some of the old churches, as Augustine is known to have done at Canterbury. In Gregory's letter of directions to Mellitus he says that the temples of idols ought not to be pulled down, but be consecrated and converted from the worship of devils. The Church of St. Peter must have been very ancient, as the legend in regard to it appears in Jocelyn of Furness, a writer of the twelfth century. Bishop Ælfric, who died in 1038, gave in his will a "hage into Sce Pætre binnon Lunden."[180] A beautifully written Saxon charter in the British Museum, calendared as probably of the date 1038, records the gift of a messuage in London to St. Peter's Church.[181] This church, seated at the Carfax of the city, has at the same time the most important of dedications, and took precedence, Riley tells us, over the others.

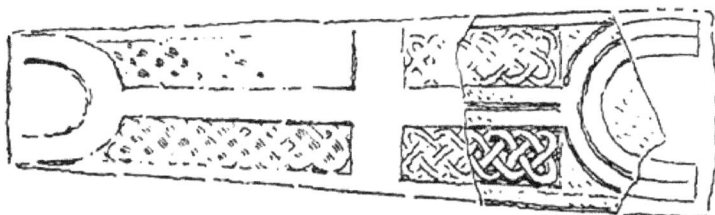

Fig. 32.—Saxon Tomb from St. Benet Fink. Restored.

St. Michael, Ludgate, is referred to by Geoffrey of Monmouth in connection with Cadwaladr: "They also built a church under it (Ludgate) in honour of St. Martin, in which divine ceremonies are celebrated for him" (Cadwaladr). It must be of early foundation when such a story could be told only some fifty years after the Conquest.

St. Mary Aldermary was so called, says Stow, because it was the oldest church dedicated to the Virgin. It is sometimes called Elde Maria Church, and certainly dates from before the Conquest, for in 1067 the Conqueror confirmed the possession of the Church of *St. Mary called Newchurch* to Westminster, and it is evident that the title Aldermary is a comparison with this New Mary. The latter as *Mary le Bow* is mentioned by William of Malmesbury as having suffered an accident in 1091. *St. Mary*, Friday Street, is mentioned in 1105; *St. Margaret*, Lothbury, in 1104.

Other pre-Conquest city churches confirmed to Westminster in the same charter of 1067 are *St. Magnus*, described as the "stone church *S. Magni Medietus*," *St. Clement* [East Cheap], and *St. Lawrence* [Pounteney].

St. Gregory.—In 1010 the body of St. Edmund was brought to "the Church of St. Gregory the Pope, which is situated by the Basilica of the Apostle Paul."[182] This dedication in the name of the Pope who sent Augustine and Mellitus from Rome is probably very ancient, and *St. Augustine's* near by on the east side of the churchyard may be as ancient. *St. Alban*, Wood Street, was said to have been a chapel of King Offa's, and is mentioned about 1077-1093 as belonging to St. Alban's Abbey.[183] The old topographers say that there was something specially ancient in the structure of this church, and Newcourt thought its origin was at least as old as the time of Athelstane.

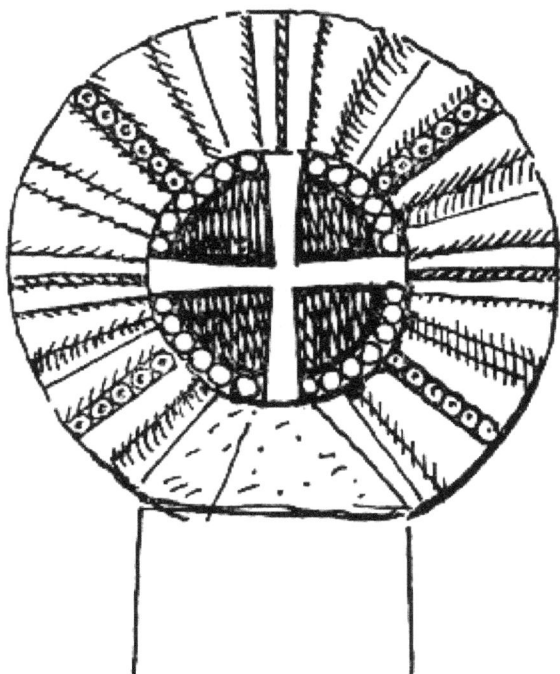

*Fig. 33.—Head of Cross from
St. John's, Walbrook.*

All Hallows [*Barking*] is said to have been given by
Riculphus and Brichtwen, his wife, to Rochester before
it passed into the hands of the Barking Nuns.[184] *All
Hallows*, Lombard Street, was given to Canterbury in 1053
by Brithmer, a citizen (Newcourt). Earl Goodwin and his
wife gave to Malmesbury the Church of *St. Nicholas* [*Acon*]
and all their houses in 1084 (Dugdale).

St. Martin's Vintry.—This church Newcourt puts at least as early as the Conqueror's time, and its name of Bereman-Church confirms this (see p. 97).

St. Martin [le Grand].—Kempe thought that this religious house was first founded long before the Conquest, and that it was only refounded just before by Ingelram. The canons of the house are mentioned amongst the tenants in chief in Domesday.[185]

St. Helen's, Bishopsgate, and *St. Alphage* were thought by Newcourt to have existed as early as the Conqueror's time, and there is ample evidence that the former was a parish church before it was attached to a house of nuns late in the twelfth century. It is mentioned in the St. Paul's documents in 1148. *St. Michael*, Cornhill, is said to have been founded before 1055. *St. Stephen*, Walbrook, was given to St. John's, Colchester, *c.* 1100.[186]

St. Botolph, Billingsgate, Stow thought, was at least as old as the Confessor's time, as the wharf by it was even then called St. Botolph's. In a part of the cartulary of Holy Trinity, Aldgate, in the Lansdowne MSS. (No. 448), *St. Augustine on the Wall*, *St. Edmund* in "Longboard" Street, *Ecclesia de Fanchurch* (which it is said had belonged to the Soc of the Cnihten Gild), *St. Lawrence in Judaismo*, *All Hallows on the Wall*, *St. Botolph extra Aldgate*, and *St. Michael, Cheapside*, are mentioned at the beginning of the twelfth century.[187]

Fig. 34.—Saxon Coffin-lid from Westminster Abbey.

Of material evidence little has survived. On the destruction of *St. Benet Fink* about fifty years ago a fragment of a Saxon grave-stone was found, which is now in the Guildhall Museum (Fig. 32). In Roach Smith's *Catalogue of London Antiquities*, No. 571, is the head of a Saxon cross ("of the tenth or eleventh century") which was found in the old burial-ground of St. John-upon-Walbrook. I am able to identify this with the cross-head in the Saxon Room at the British Museum from a sketch of Roach Smith's, which I have, which bears the same number 571 (see the diagram, Fig. 33). It has been said that Roman foundations have been found under some of the churches.[188]

Several of the churches outside the walls can be traced back so far as to make it probable that they were founded before the Conquest.

The Assise of 1189(?), speaking of a fire in the first year of Stephen (1136), says it burnt from London Bridge to *S.*

Clementis Danorum; in a charter of Henry II. this church is called *S. Clementis quæ dicitur Dacorum* (Dugdale, under "Temple"). It was still earlier the subject of a charter of the Conqueror's (see p. 85). According to M. of Westminster the body of Harold I., buried at Westminster, was dug up in 1040 and thrown into the Thames, "but it was found and buried by the Danish people in the cemetery of the Danes"—"at S. Clement's," says R. Diceto, the London historian who wrote in the twelfth century. This is probably the cemetery of the Danes who were killed in London in Ethelred's reign. M. of Westminster (under 1012) says many of the Danes fled to a certain church in the city, where they were all murdered. Stow says they were slain in a place called the Church of the Danes.

St. Mary le Strand.—Here Becket held his first cure. His biographer FitzStephen calls it *S. Mariæ Littororiam. St. Andrew's*, Holborn, is mentioned in the somewhat doubtful charter dated 951 (see p. 60). *St. Bridget*, Fleet Street, was also of early foundation (Stow). *St. Sepulchre's* is mentioned in the twelfth century.[189] Of the monasteries in the neighbourhood, *Barking* was founded in the seventh century, *Westminster* not later than the tenth, and *Bermondsey*, the fine new church of which is mentioned in Domesday, was probably only refounded by Alwyn Childe. A "monasterium" in Southwark mentioned in Domesday may be *St. Olave*, which is spoken of as early as 1096.[190]

All the manors round about London probably had churches before the Conquest, although the only one we can be certain of is that of St. Pancras, as the place is called by that name in Domesday. Stepney Church is said to have been rebuilt by Dunstan. It still contains a small sculpture of the Crucifixion, which is probably eleventh-century work. What these little churches were like we may know from the illustrations of the Saxon church at Kingston which was destroyed at the beginning of this century, and the log church at Greenstead, Essex, which still stands.

A story in the *Heimskringla* shows how London was early celebrated for its number of churches and London Bridge for its crowds.[191] A French cripple dreamt that an angel appeared to him and said, "Fare thou to Olaf's church, the one that is in London." Thereafter he awoke and fared to seek Olaf's church, and at last he came to London Bridge and there asked the folk of the city to tell him where was Olaf's church. But they answered and said that there were many more churches there than they might wot to what man they were hallowed. But a little thereafter came a man to him who asked whither he was bound, and the cripple told him, and sithence said that man, "We twain shall fare both to the church of Olaf, for I know the way thither." Therewith they fared over the Bridge, and went along the street which led to Olaf's church. But when they came to the lich-gate then strode that one over the threshold of the gate, but the cripple rolled in over it and straightway rose up a whole man. But when he looked around him his fellow-farer was vanished.

CHAPTER VIII

THE GUILDHALL—LONDON STONE—TOWN BELL AND FOLKMOTE

It is so sure a Stone that that is upon sette,

For though some have it thretce

With menases grym and greette

Yet hurt had it none.

Fabyan.

The Guildhall is frequently spoken of in the thirteenth century; for instance, the Assise of Buildings of 1212 was given from "Gilde Hall." Mr. Price, its historian, shows that at this time it must have stood near the west end of the present hall. This agrees with Stow, who says that it "of old time" stood on the east side of Aldermansbury, and adds that the latter was so named from the "court there kept in their bury or court hall now called the Guildhall." Guildhall Yard was in 1294, as now, to the east of St. Laurence.[192] Giraldus Cambrensis tells us under 1191 how a multitude of the citizens met in Aula Publica, which takes its name from the custom of drinking there. This burgmote at the Guildhall in 1191 was probably the greatest event in London's history, resulting in the removal of Longchamp and the establishment of the mayor and commune.[193] "Aldermanesbury" may be traced back to early in the twelfth century, and the name carries the Guildhall with it. Mr. Round points out that the *Terra Gialle* mentioned in the St. Paul's document, *c.* 1130, refers to the Guildhall,[194] and when further we find that a *Gildhalla burgensium* at Dover appears in Domesday we can hardly doubt that the foundation of the London hall dates from the time of the Frith Gilds. In the laws of Athelstane it was ordained by the "bishops and reeves of London" that the people should be numbered in *hyndens* (tens), and that "every month the hynden men and those who directed the tithings should gather together for bytt filling, ... and let those twelve men have their refection together and deal the remains for the love of God."[195]

The principle, says Dr. Sharpe, of each man being responsible for the behaviour of his neighbour, which Alfred established, was carried a step further in London under Athelstane in the formation of Peace Gilds, the members of which were to meet once a month at an ale-drinking in their Gildhall.[196] Similar "Gild ale-drinkings" are spoken of in the *Heimskringla*, and we are there told in regard to the establishment of a "Great Gild," that before it there were "turn-about drinkings." All this goes together perfectly with what Giraldus says of the Guildhall of London being named from the fellowship drinkings there. He who drank to any one, Geoffrey of Monmouth tells us, said, "Wacht heil"; and he that pledged him answered, "Drinc heil."

London Stone.—The first mayor of London (from 1191) was, as the Chronicle of the Mayors and Sheriffs tells us, Henry FitzEylwin of Londene-stone. An old marginal note in the *Liber Trinitatis* says that "Leovistan was the father of Alwin the father of Henry the Mayor, whose first charter is in the priory of Tortingtone."[197] The association of London Stone with city history probably rests in great part on the fact of the mayor's residence having been near to it. Thomas Stopleton traces, in an introduction to the *Liber de Antiquis Legibus*,[198] the property and descendants of FitzAlwin. The town house of the mayor was just to the north of St. Swithin's Church, which was attached to the property. It was bequeathed to Tortington Priory by Robert Aquillon, son of the first mayor's grand-daughter. In Dr. Sharpe's *Calendar of Wills* it appears that Sir Robert Aguylun left his "mansione" in St. Swithin's parish, together with the patronage of the church, to Tortington Priory in 1285. At the Dissolution it was granted to the Earl of Oxford. Stow says that Tortington Inn, Oxford Place, by London Stone, was on the north side of St. Swithin's Church and churchyard, with a fair garden to the west running down to Walbrook. It was "a fair and large builded house sometime pertaining to the prior of

Tortington, since to the earls of Oxford, and now to Sir John Hart, Alderman." Munday adds, "*now* to Master Humphrey Smith, Alderman." At this point I visited Oxford Place and St. Swithin's Lane, and it seemed evident that the Salters' Hall stood on the site of Tortington Inn. Further, on turning to Herbert's *History of the Companies,* I found that the Salters' Company purchased of Captain George Smith in 1641 the town inn of the priors of Tortington by the description of "the great house called London Stone, or Oxford House." The chain of evidence for the site of FitzAlwin's house thus seems complete.

The mysterious monument, London Stone, now represented by a small rude fragment preserved a few yards away from its original site, has probably borne its present name for a millenium, and its mere name shows it to have had some institutional importance.

London. Candlewick Street. Enter Jack Cade and the rest, and strikes his staff on London Stone.

Cade. Now is Mortimer lord of this city and here sitting upon London Stone I charge, ... and now henceforward it shall be treason for any that calls me other than Lord Mortimer.—*King Henry VI.*

Shakespeare here accurately follows Holinshed's Chronicle as to the events of 1450. About 1430 the Stone is mentioned by Harding, who tells us that it marked the eastern boundary of London as built by King Lud, whose palace was at Ludgate. About 1400-30 Lydgate, in the *London Lickpenny*, wrote: "Then forth I went by London Stone, throughout all the Canwick Street."[199]

The *Liber Trinitatis* says that a great fire in the time of Ralf the prior of Holy Trinity, 1148-67, burnt from the house of Ailwardin nigh London Stone to Aldgate and St. Paul's. Of the Stone itself Stow says: "The same has long continued there, namely since (or rather before) the Conquest, for in the end of a Gospel book given to Christ Church in Canterbury by Athelstane I find noted of lands in London belonging to the said church one parcel described to lie near unto London Stone."[200]

Holinshed says that the Kentish captain came from the White Hart in Southwark and "strooke his sword on London Stone, saying, Now is Mortimer lord of this city." Mr. Coote has claimed that this must be an ancient ceremonial, at the same time advancing the impossible (after Wren's acceptance of it as Roman) theory that the stone was a part of the house of the first mayor.[201] But I have come over to this view so far as to think it possible that its civic importance originated in its association with the house of the first mayor. According to Stow, "some have said this stone to be set as a mark in the middle of the city—some others have said the same to be set for the making of payment by debtors to their creditors, till of later times payments were more usually made at the font in Paul's Church and now most commonly at the Royal Exchange." Mr. Gomme, citing Brandon, says that London Stone entered into municipal procedure, as when the defendant in the Lord Mayor's Court had to be summoned from that spot, and when proclamations and other important business of like nature were transacted there; and comparing Cade's action with customs elsewhere, he seems to suggest that it was the centre for the assembly of the Saxon folkmotes. But the proximity of the mayor's house, in which courts might have been held, gives reason enough for its being made use of as a place of proclamation.

The legend given by Harding is that "Lud, king of Britain, built from London Stone to Ludgate and called that part Ludstowne." Here we get a clue to its name London Stone, and the idea accounts for its having been to some extent the palladium of the city, of which it seems to have been regarded as the sacred and immovable foundation stone. Stow says, "On the south side of the High Street near unto the channel is pitched upright a great stone called London Stone, fixed in the ground very deep, fastened with bars of iron, and otherwise so strongly set that if carts do run against it through negligence the wheels be broken and the stone itself unshaken." The lines from Fabyan which head this chapter refer to this same idea of stability, and evidently imply that the stone was looked on as a talisman. Strype says that before the fire of London it was worn down to a stump. But it is "now" handsomely cased with stone "to shelter and defend the old venerable one, yet so as it might be seen." An architect, writing to the *Gentleman's Magazine* in 1798, says: "It has often been called the symbol of the great city's quiet state, from its being always believed to be fixed to its everlasting seat." This idea of a stone of foundation has many parallels.

It was evidently a monolith, and from what Shakespeare says of Cade sitting on it, it would seem in his time not to have been more than 3 or 4 feet high above ground. Wren's son says "London Stone, as is generally supposed, was a pillar in the manner of the Milliarium Aureum at Rome, from whence the account of their miles began, but the Surveyor [Sir Christopher] was of opinion, *by reason of the large foundation*, it was rather some more considerable monument in the Forum, for in the adjoining ground on the south side, upon digging for cellars after the great fire, were discovered some pavements and other extensive remains of Roman workmanship and buildings."[202] Wren was an expert observer with a perfect knowledge of the Roman level in the city, and Dr. Woodward says he had made a special observation of the Roman remains in the city and promised an account of them. His evidence must be held sufficient to prove that the stone was of Roman origin, but was no recognisable part of a building such as a column. It was Camden who first suggested that it was a "miliary like that in the Forum of Rome," being at the "centre in the longest diameter of the city." Grant Allen thought it was an early Celtic monument preserved by the Romans. As to Mr. Coote's view that it might have been part of FitzAlwin's house, which seems to be adopted also by Mr. Round, it has also to be pointed out that the house was certainly to the north of the street, while the Stone was on the south, and St. Swithin's Church intervened.

Town Bell and Folkmote.—An institution which must have dated from the time of the English occupation was the great assembly of all freemen in Folkmote, the final court which survives to-day in form at the election of a sovereign, when the Commons, who should have free access, are asked for their assent. Stephen was elected at the ordinary Folkmote of London, and the charter of Henry I. recognises the assembly as an existing institution. The place of assembly within historical times was the market of St. Paul's (*Forum Sancto Paulo*), at the east of the cathedral against Cheap, marked by St. Paul's Cross.

The Chronicle of the Mayors and Sheriffs tells how Henry III. in 1257 ordered the sheriffs to convene the Folkmote "at St. Paul's Cross, to make inquiry of the commons" as to certain customs, when the populace answered "with loud shouts of Nay, nay, nay." The position held by St. Paul's Cross in civic customs in later times is thus accounted for.

It was no mere adjunct to the cathedral, but the rostrum of London, the Market Cross at the end of Cheap. Just by it rose the city belfry (*Berefridam*), which contained the great town bell. Such a Beffroi is an acknowledged mark of communal liberties, and we can understand the traditional feeling which was stirred when under Edward VI. it was destroyed. Even at this day it is the Lord Mayor who orders the Great Bell of St. Paul's to be rung on such an occasion as the death of the late Queen. Probably the "mote-bell" summoned the citizens in Saxon times, as we know it did in the thirteenth century. Dugdale says the first mention he found of the bell tower was *temp.* Henry I., when the schoolmaster of St. Paul's was granted a house "at the corner of the Turret (id est the Clochier); but I suppose it was a thing of much greater antiquity, for upon a writ issued 15 Edward I., it was certified that the citizens of ancient time held the Folkmote there and rang the bell to summon the people." The *Gesta Stephani* records how the citizens assembled at the ringing of the city bells and expelled the Empress Matilda.

The *Heimskringla* tells of Olaf the Quiet, the contemporary of Edward the Confessor, that "in his days the cheaping steads of Norway hove up much.... King Olaf let set up the Great Gild at Nidoyce and many others in the cheaping towns, but formerly there were turn-about drinkings. Then was Town-boon[203] the great bell of the turn-about drinkings in Nidoyce. The Drinking Brothers let build there Margaret's stone church." One day Olaf was merry in the Great Gild, then spake his men, "It is joy to us, lord, that thou art so merry." He answered, "Your freedom is my glee."

We need a town bell in London. We might set it up to Alfred's memory.

CHAPTER IX

THE GOVERNMENT OF EARLY LONDON

The kynges chambre of custom men this calle.—
Lydgate.

The Kings Peace.—When Alfred took over London it must have been in the main a decayed Roman city. In giving the great burh into the hands of the Mercian Ealdorman, Ethered, he was but restoring its capital to Mercia, but he must also, and mainly, have had in view the need for providing means of defence to the frontier fortress of the March country. Even so, alongside of a supreme military rule a more domestic organisation of a customary nature must have been carried on or reintroduced. It is probable that this, following the shire model, was constituted with hundreds or wards; the people met in wardmote and folkmote, and the king was represented by a Sheriff or Portreeve. London, however, was and remained pre-eminently a royal burh, and must have shared in all the characteristics of the burhs, drawing on certain shires for upholding its defences, having a Witan, coining money, having special privileges as to residence, gilds, and markets, and being subject to the King's Peace. As to the contributions for defence, Dr. Maitland, as we have seen on p. 105, says, "There were shires or districts which from of old owed work of this kind to Londonbury."[204] Regarding the King's Peace, it was provided by the laws that every crime committed, in a street which ran right through the city and likewise without the walls for a distance of over a league, was a crime against the king. In London the man who was guilty had to pay the king's burh-bryce of five pounds. The burh was to be sacred from private quarrels—"the King's house-peace prevails in the streets."[205] Some such fact as this is probably the origin of that almost mythical phrase applied to the city by Lydgate and earlier writers—"the king's chamber of London." It is to this aspect as the great model burh that the Saxon laws of London printed by Thorpe refer.

There must have been a Burh Witan meeting periodically. A Crediton charter of 1018 was made known to the Witans of Exeter, Barnstaple, Lidford, and Totness, *i.e.* the Devonshire burhs. The Witan was thus a court of record or witness. Probably the Hustings court is a form of the same assembly.

———

Portreeves.—Fabyan says that at the coming of William the Conqueror and before, the rulers of the city were named Portgreves. "These of old time, with the laws and customs then used within the city, were registered in a book called Domysday in Saxon tongue then used, but of later days when the said laws and customs altered and changed and for consideration that the said book was of small hand and sore defaced and hard to be read or understood, it was the less set by, so that it was embezzled or lost, so that the remembrance of such rulers as were before the days of Richard the First (*i.e.* the institution of the mayoralty) were lost and forgotten."

The office of Portreeve probably goes back nearly to the first settlement of the English. Bishop Stubbs, speaking generally of town organisation, says, "The presiding magistrate was the gerefa." The king's wic-gerefa in Lundonwic is mentioned in the Saxon Laws of *c.* 685 (Thorpe).[206] The charter of the Conqueror ran, "I, King William, greet William the Bishop and Gosfregth the Portreeve," and two of the Confessor's charters were addressed to bishop and portreeve. In the *Judicia Civitatis Londoniæ* of Athelstane a reference is found to "the bishops and gereves that to London borough belong." Norton says that these Laws show that in Athelstane's time the bishops and reeves were the chief magistrates of London, and they likewise presided at county courts with a jurisdiction precisely similar. This conjunction of the spiritual and temporal powers probably explains why it is that St. Paul's has always been linked in such a special way to the Guildhall. At St. Paul's was kept the city banner, grants of money from city funds are made for its repair, and the mayor is a trustee of the church. This dual control seems to bear the mark of Alfred's thought. The Portreeve certainly represented the king, and was responsible for the farm of the city. In the *Blickling Homilies* Agrippa is called Nero's Burhgerefa. It would seem as if the bishop represented the collective citizens. Mr. Round has recently shown that the Portreeve disappeared in the Sheriff or Vicecomes of London and Middlesex. The Waltham Chronicle says that the Conqueror placed Geoffrey de Mandeville in the shoes of Esegar the Staller, and Mr. Round conjectures that this Geoffrey is the actual "Gosfregth Portirefan" to whom the Conqueror's charter was addressed. He also points out how the Sheriff had the custody of the Tower; and in this we may find a further suggestion as to the probability of a connection between the Portsoken of the Cnihten Gild, the Portreeve, and the pre-Conquest citadel. Mr. Round seems not to have known that his suppositions were all taken for granted by Stow, who calls the Portreeve of the Conqueror's charter Godfrey, and then writes, "In the reign of the said Conqueror, Godfrey de Magnaville was Portgrave (or Sheriff); ... these Portgraves (after the Conquest) are also called Vicecounties or Sheriffs." Mr. Round shows that the Sheriff, and by inference the Portreeve, represented London and Middlesex taken together. "The city of London was never severed from the rest of the shire. As far back as we can trace them they are one and indivisible."[207] The author just quoted accounts for this distinction between London and other county towns by the relative importance of London; but I cannot think, as before suggested, that Middlesex was

172

not specially dependant on London, and probably Ethered's authority as commandant of the great burh extended over Middlesex. The acquisition of the farm of the county by the city may be an echo of this.

Stow gave a list of the Portreeves from the time of the Conquest. In the additional matter printed by Hearne in his edition of William of Newbury is given, from a register of Holy Trinity, Aldgate, what must be another copy of Stow's authority for the early sheriffs for which he cited a book "sometime belonging to St. Albans." Both may come from the old book called "*Domysday*," by Fabyan. In the list given by Hearne the names are much less corrupt than in Stow's list; and as it ends with the year 1222 it must have been an early document. The Chronicle of the Mayors and Sheriffs gives still another list from the first year of Richard onward, and so far as they overlap, the three can be compared.[208]

According to Hearne's list the principal governor of the citizens of London in the days of the Confessor was Wulfgar, called *Portshyreve*. In the reign of William Rufus, Geoffrey de Magnaville was *vicecomes* and R. del Parc *præpositus*. In the time of Henry I. came Hugo de Boch' [Bochland], v., and Leofstan, p. Albericus de Ver, v., and Robertus de Berquereola, p., followed.

In the reign of Stephen we have the names of Gilbertus Beket, v., and Andreas Buchuint, p. Under Henry II. Petrus filius Walteri was vicecomes, then Johannes filius Nigelli, then Ernulfus Buchel, then Willelmus filius Isabellæ, the last of whom was buried in Holy Trinity Church, Aldgate.

Richard I. was crowned September 1189. In his days first began to be two vicecomites at the same time, who were usually chosen 21st September. In his first year they were Henricus Cornhill and Ricardus filius Reneri.

The Chronicle of the Mayors and Sheriffs begins with these same two names of what it calls the "first sheriffs of London, in the first year of the reign of King Richard." It, however, places this in 1188; then follow other pairs of names as in Stow, but all a year earlier, till 1206, when Serlo le Mercer and Henry de Saint Auban are interpolated, probably by mistake, unless they merely occupied the position for the portion of a year.

From the Pipe Rolls and St. Paul's documents many more facts as to the sheriffs can be gathered, and Mr. Round's article on the "Early Administration of London," in his *Geoffrey de Mandeville*, must be taken as the starting-point for any complete inquiry.

The first Mayor.—The institution of the mayoralty is put in the year 1188 by the Chronicle of the Mayors and Sheriffs. In Hearne's list, under 1208, is entered Henry son of Alwin son of Leofstan, first of the mayors of London, who were chosen St. Edward's day (13th October).

174

Stow agrees with the chronicle, and puts the institution of the mayoralty in the first year of Richard I.; but under 1208 we find an echo of the version as printed by Hearne, for Stow makes King John, in this year, grant the citizens a patent "to chuse to themselves a mayor." Be the explanation of this what it may, contemporary documents show that Fitzalwin was already known as mayor in 1193; he probably took up the office in 1191.

Stow tells us that the first mayor was Henry Fitzalwin Fitzleofstan of London Stone, and there is ample confirmation that his father was called Alwin. That his grandfather was Leofstan, Stow must have learnt from the list of sheriffs as in the copy printed by Hearne.

There is some confusion between many Leofstans and Alwins, one of whom signs as moneyer the coins of Henry II. about 1160—Alwin on Lund. Mr. Round has shown that in 1165 a Henry Fitzailwin Fitzleofstan with Alan his brother were landholders, apparently in Essex.[209] Stow says that Leofstan was a goldsmith; but here he may be confusing another Leofstan, as this fact does not seem to have been given in the list of sheriffs. Munday contradicted Stow as to Mayor Henry's grave being at Holy Trinity, and says he was buried at St. Mary Bothaw, and not as "avowed by Mr. Stow." Stow's authority, however, must have been this same list of sheriffs, for that notes that "he was buried at the entrance to the chapter of the Church of Holy Trinity, under a marble slab." Mr. Round has done much to clear up the history of our first mayor in the *Dictionary of National Biography*, the *Archæological Journal*, and his *Commune of London*; but every detail is valuable of the head of the City Republic of whom the citizens said, "Come what will, in London we will never have another king except our mayor, Henry Fitailwin of London Stone."[210] Henry was mayor for nearly twenty years, and was followed in 1212 by Roger Fitz Alan—can he have been Henry's nephew?

Hustings.—This court is mentioned in the charter of Henry I., and in a passage in the so-called Laws of the Confessor the Hustings Court is said to have been founded of old in imitation of and to continue the royal customs of Great Troy. FitzStephen also repeats the legend that the laws of the city were derived from the Trojans, and the passage from the Laws of the Confessor was copied into the *Liber Albus*. It was suggested nearly three centuries since by Munday, that "Troy weight" is the ancient standard weight of London, and carries on the legend of Brutus to this day; but this is not borne out by the facts, although it is frequently reasserted, as in Brewer's *Phrase and Fable*. Munday says, "The weight used for gold and silver called Troy weight was in the time of the Saxons called 'the Hustings weight of London,' and kept there in the Hustings. So an ancient record in the Book of Ramsey (sect. 32, 127): 'I Æthelgiva Countess, etc., bequeath two silver cups of twelve marks of the Hustings weight of London.'"[211] This is interesting as an early notice of the Hustings Court, which is thought by some to have originated under the Danish rule; but the word "Thing" occurs in one of the earliest English laws. It was a Court of Record; the best account of it is given by Dr. Sharpe in his *Calendar of Wills*.

The Court of Hustings was not, it appears, necessarily associated with the Guildhall. A Ramsey Charter of 1114-30 speaks of a purchase of a house being completed "in the presence of the whole Court of Hustings of London in the house of Alfwine, son of Leofstan."[212]

CHAPTER X

LONDINIUM

"London was built on the first spot going up the river where any considerable tract of dry land touches the stream. It is a tract of good gravel, well supplied with water, not liable to flooding, and not commanded by neighbouring higher ground."—Lord Avebury, *Scenery of England*.

From the standing-ground of what is known of London in the Middle Ages, I have endeavoured to reach back towards Londinium Augusta. To set out adequately all the data that we have for reconstructing the Roman city would require a treatise from a specialist. I can only venture here a rapid glance in conclusion at the more salient features of the ancient town. Much in recent years has been written as to a still earlier London than that included within the circuit of Roman walls which held what is now known as the City. It is at once evident that the early city must have had a nucleus and a greater density in one part than in others; and every evidence goes to show that this earliest centre was situated on the east side of the Walbrook at the head of London Bridge. We have the facts of the position of the Bridge itself, and the suitability of the site; the evidence that important buildings were densely packed in this district, while outside of it they were more and more scattered; and also that no graves have been found within this area. Mr. Roach Smith thought that certain remnants of thick walls found near Cannon Street in the south and Cornhill in the north were probably parts of earlier city walls. He says: "Here and there during excavations, walls of great thickness, which may be referred to walls of circumvallation, were intersected. The extraordinary sub-structures which were cut through in Bush Lane and Scott's Yard indicate a south-east boundary wall with a flanking tower. In Cornhill another thick wall which seemed to point towards the Bank of England was met with." Then, in a passage already referred to above, he concludes that old London Bridge pointed to the axis of this earlier Londinium, the centre or carfax of which was at the intersection of Gracechurch Street and East-Cheap. He was inclined to place the earlier north wall along the course of Cornhill and Leadenhall Street, the east wall in the direction of Billiter Street and Mark Lane, the south in the line of Thames streets, and the west on the eastern bank of the Walbrook—an irregular square with four gates, corresponding with Bridge Gate, Bishop's Gate, Ludgate, and Aldgate.[213]

Fig. 35.—Roman Pavement. Drawn in situ by Fairholt, 1854.

Possibly Wren had found some remnant of such an earlier north wall, for he put the northward extent of the city along Cheapside and in line with Cornhill. This earlier north wall seems to have been again found about 1897, in which year Mr. Williamson sent the following passage to the Middlesex and Herts *Notes and Queries*:—"Very close to St. Peter's-upon-Cornhill, *Roman* walls of immense thickness have been discovered, proceeding in a westerly direction from Leadenhall Market under the Woolpack Tavern in Gracechurch Street along St. Peter's Alley, a few feet on the south side of the churchyard of St. Peter's, continuing under the banking-house of Messrs. Prescott, Dimsdale, & Co. (50 Cornhill), *supposed* to continue under the roadway of

Cornhill, and appearing again in the foundations of the new building now being erected on the *north* side of Cornhill (No. 70) for the Union Bank of Australia. For what purpose, is it conjectured, were these walls at Leadenhall and Cornhill built?" By the aid of this valuable observation, I think that the concluding question may be safely answered by the theory of earlier walls.

Mr. Loftie has brought forward a suggestion, or rather stated a conclusion, that there was in the earlier days a walled castrum, like Richborough, at the head of London Bridge, reaching northwards to the "Langbourne." It is not usual to seat such a post on a steep hill-side, it would be curious to pass all the Bridge traffic through it, and, finally, I have not found a vestige of foundation for its existence—it is a castrum in the air.[214]

It may be held for certain that when Tacitus, writing of the insurrection of A.D. 62, spoke of London as a wealthy and important place, no walls existed, for of the still more important Camalodunum he tells us that it had no defences, and the garrison could only fortify themselves in the temple. "The Roman generals," he says, "neglecting the useful, embellished the province, but took no care for its defence."

However, it is reasonable to suppose that the chief centres would have been protected a little later under the very thorough policy of Agricola, if these shortcomings were so noticed when Tacitus wrote; and it is the opinion of Mr.

Haverfield, our best authority on things Roman, that the walls of the sister city of Silchester, now so well known to us, go back to this time.

I cannot think that the greater wall of London dates back to the first century, but it has never been proved to be later.

Fig. 36.—Roman Brick inscribed London.

Fig. 37.—Inscription from Roman Brick.

Fragments of sculpture, themselves not very early, have been found in portions of the wall, yet the Camomile Street bastion and other similar places might be additions and repairs; and some late fragments from the south wall found by Roach Smith seem to have come from its foundation (Figs. 24 and 25).

If it is difficult to offer any convincing argument as to the age of the wall of London, it is possible to get a general idea of the walled city and its neighbourhood with some vividness and accuracy. We have the great tidal river, the background of forest, and the nearer fen-lands, which seem to have almost insulated the site. There is the great white posting-road from Canterbury and Dover, and, more remotely, from Rome, Lyons, Chalons, Auxerre, Troyes, Rheims, Amiens, Boulogne, striking straight from point to point. On its course are villas, like one just discovered in Greenwich Park. The road dips towards the river, and passes over the drained and banked marshes to the Surrey suburb. There is a gate-tower at the end of the Bridge, then comes the long and narrow passage over the strong, swift river to the grey walls of Londinium. Along the river-front are several wharves formed of timbering, to the left is the creek of the little river which ran under the west walls, and, still further west, some water-side villas.[215] Entering the city the street ascends steeply towards the north gate; others, parallel to its course, lead to two other gates in the north wall, and two chief routes traverse the city longitudinally from west gate to east gate, and from west postern to east postern. A bridge[216] over the Walbrook gives good reason why the street lines in the eastern half of the city converge toward this point. The area extending from the north-gate street to the bank of the Walbrook is covered with the principal buildings closely packed together.[217] Beyond this central mass of buildings stand isolated villas in gardens and orchards. In the open belt of ground outside the walls, and along the roads, west, north, and east, are cemeteries, the graves marked with sarcophagi and sculptured headstones, some of imported marble. A theatre somewhat similar to those at Dorchester, Cirencester, and Silchester is situated without the west gate, being excavated in the steep bank of the rivulet between it and the city wall.[218]

Fig. 38.—*Roman Tomb, from outside of the East Walls.*
Restored.

Fig. 39.—*Inscription from Roman Tomb.*

Within the walls the city is adorned by more than
one bronze statue. The sculptured ornaments of the public
buildings are somewhat rude and ponderous, but the
dwellings are furnished with numerous imported works of

art, such as bronze statuettes, bowls of red Samian ware, and very beautiful coloured glass vessels of the *millefiore* kind. The rooms have their walls painted in bright colours with birds, flowers, and figures, and imitations of porphyry and verde antique, while a few are cased with thin slabs of marble. The pavements are patterned mosaic, and raised above hot air chambers; lead pipes supply water, the windows are glazed, and the roofs without are covered with red pantiles. So far there seem to be authentic data for such a picture. It would be vain to attempt in many instances to assign the fragments found in excavations to particular buildings. Roach Smith, however, was of opinion that a large fragment sculptured with the three seated goddesses, the *Deae Matres*, found in Hart Street, Crutched Friars, and now in the Guildhall, "stood on the outside of a temple dedicated to these popular divinities."

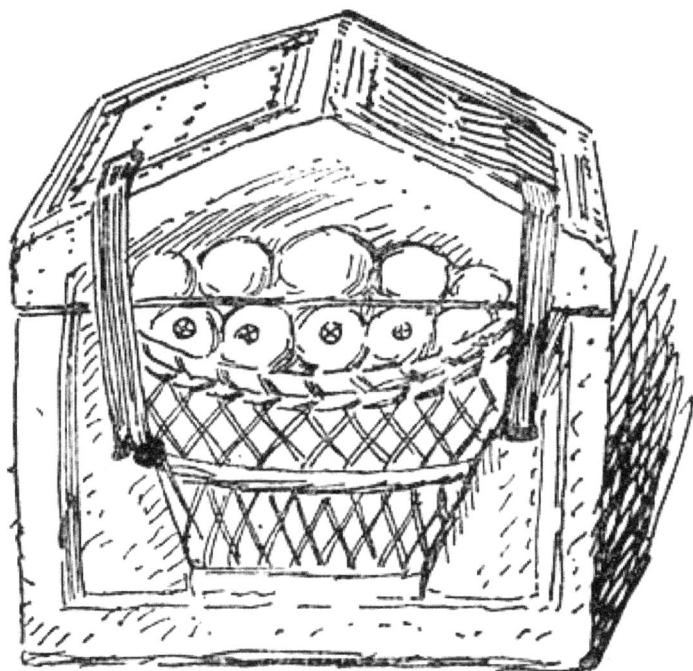

Fig. 40.—End of a Roman Tomb found in London.

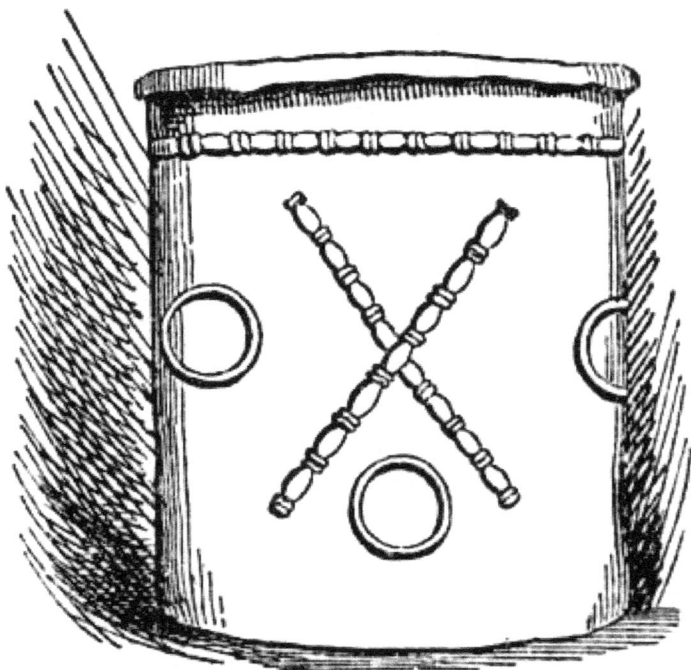

Fig. 41.—Leaden Cist.

Fig. 42.—Plate of figured Glass for Decoration.

Fig. 43.—Roman Inscription.

The illustration of a tomb is made up from fragments in the British Museum found in the east wall (Figs. <u>38 and 39</u>).

A large stone, about two feet high, found fifty years ago below Clement's Lane, Lombard Street, bearing "a few letters of the sounding words PROVINCIA BRITANNIAE," was thought by the same authority to have stood above a civil basilica. This most important inscription was lodged at the Guildhall, but has disappeared. I have Roach Smith's original sketch of it, and a letter asking Fairholt to go and draw it more carefully. But in his *Roman London* he complains that it could not be found. Fortunately, there is a second careful drawing of the stone in the Archer Collection at the British Museum, and from this my figure is made.[219]

Following the model of Silchester, it is quite probable that a Christian church stood in a main street on such a site as the present St. Peter's upon Cornhill. The Forum, as has been said, probably lay north of London Stone, which may have been the golden milestone of London. Wren thought that the Prætorium occupied the ground between the two west gates; but the Tower site seems even more probable.

Bagford refers to the discovery of some Roman water-pipes in Creed Lane after the fire, which were "carried round a bath that was built in a round form with niches at an equal distance for seats."

It has been noticed that the masonry of the walls of the Roman houses seems to have finished not far above ground as if in preparation for timbering; other indications of this have been found, and a rough scratching of a house on a tile shows timber construction. This has recently been confirmed by the discovery at Silchester of houses which had timbered framing covered with clay daubing over wattle work, the outside surface being ornamented with zigzag patterns like mediæval pargeting, all of brick-red colour.

Before the Roman forces were drawn back to the heart of the empire, London seems to have grown into the position of British Metropolis. Its position in regard to the arterial roads when the itinerary was compiled, shows how it tended to take precedence over the more military centres. Moreover, while the mint marks of one or two British cities appear on coins earlier than the mark of London, in Constantinian days London is the only British city where money seems to have been coined.[220] In the last days of the occupation the city had acquired the name of Augusta. We cannot doubt that the Roman soldiers drawn away to protect their lines of communication marched Romeward with the intention of returning again to the city by the Thames when the barbarian Germans and Goths had been thrust back into their woods and plains; yet the day of Rome was done, and their retreat was itself an incident in the advance of a new age.

APPENDIX

ON MATERIALS FOR THE CONSTRUCTION OF
MAPS OF EARLY LONDON

In bringing this topographical essay to a conclusion, it may be desirable to note a few observations on the materials we possess for making a map of early London, the reconstruction of which, with considerable fulness and accuracy, is possible. We have in the Survey of Leeke, made directly after the great fire, and engraved on two sheets by Vertue from a parchment original, now in the MS. room of the British Museum (5415. E.I.), an admirable starting-point. Even the widths of the streets are figured on this plan, and the forms of St. Paul's and the other old churches are given with fair precision. It is entitled "An Exact Survey of the Streets, Lanes, and Churches, comprehended within the Ruins of the City of London; first described in six platts in December, Anno Domini, 1666. By John Leeke.... And here reduced into one entire platt by John Leeke." This parchment was engraved by Hollar to a smaller scale, with the unburnt portions of the city added in isometrical projection. On this plan the ward boundaries are carefully laid down. As to the ground-plan of the portions left uninjured by the fire, we can supplement Leeke's Survey by the plan Wren made for reconstructing the city, now at Oxford, which shows the streets and churches of the uninjured areas; and from Ogilvie's large map, made only a few years later, details, such as the block-plans of the churches in the unburnt part, can be filled in with greater accuracy. From Faithorne's map, 1658, some additional facts, especially as to Southwark and the suburbs, can be obtained, as it is of large extent. [221] Putting all these together, we have an exact map of London as it existed at the moment of the fire. Afterwards a few modifications were made in the streets, but the plan of old London remained practically unchanged till Southwark Bridge was built and Queen Street made to lead to it.

We can now check our plan and add to the names of the streets from Stow's perambulation of every street and alley, and his account of ward boundaries and parishes. Further than this, however, we have in the remarkably clear plot of the city given in Braun and Hogenburghe's *Civitates Orbis Terrarum* (1572), a survey of the city as it existed about 1570. It is often said that this view *must* date back to 1561 at least, as St. Paul's spire, which was burnt in that year, is shown in it. But as it was known to be the intention to rebuild this famous spire at once, it seems probable that a view even in the interim would not leave it out. It is not quite certain who drew this admirable map. In the preface to a copy of the book which I have examined, George Braun of Cologne, January 1, 1575, speaks of the admirable industry of the

194

painter Hogenburghe, and the living portraitures he had so carefully painted, so that the cities may be seen at a glance more easily than in reality. On comparing the prospects of other cities, it looks almost certain that London was drawn by the same hand which drew Paris, Brussels, etc. Hofnagle, who it is thought may have made this prospect, is known to have been in England in or before 1571. It is to be remarked in this connection that the plan of London is not numbered with the rest of the plates; it is marked A, and put in at the beginning of the series as if it came to hand late.

This valuable map, whoever it may have been drawn by, and whatever may be its exact date, is delineated according to a method which is still made use of at times—the buildings, trees, and other details being figured in perspective. This has resulted in giving the whole such a pictorial character, that the correctly planned basis is not at first apparent. I have not seen it pointed out that it is properly a map and not a view, and this method of projection may be what Braun refers to in the preface cited above. About this same time William Smith, the herald, made some drawings of cities; and on one of Bristol, which is drawn according to the same method as the London map we are now considering, he writes:— "Bristow, measured and laid in Platforme by me, W. Smith, at my being in Bristow the 30 and 31 July Ano Dni 1568" (Sloane MSS. 2596). Pictorial views of cities had been known for centuries; this "laying in platform" is, however, new. We may suppose that Smith, the Rouge Dragon, was not the first to make use of this method in his Survey of Bristol, and that there must even at this time have existed such a plan of London; it may also be pointed out that Smith's MS. *view* of London, which may, however, have been made later than the one of Bristol, is plainly founded on Braun's plan, or on some original used in common. Bagford speaks of having seen a single sheet on copper, from Temple Bar to St. Katharine's and the Bank-side Southwark, which seemed to him the best of old London and perhaps the most ancient.

It is necessary to notice the large woodcut prospect usually called Aggas' plan, if only to criticise this ascription, which is accepted in the *Dictionary of National Biography*. It is plain on comparing it with Braun's plan that one of them is copied from the other, or a common original source, and this relation is made more certain when we notice that the large woodcut, which I shall call the Anonymous plan, has been cut down at the margins, and that it must originally have included Westminster and St. Katharine's exactly like Braun's. As the Anonymous woodcut plan is far inferior in workmanship to the other, and as it was still being printed from in the seventeenth century, there seems to be some likelihood that it is the copy, and yet, as we shall see, a "Large Mappe" existed before 1580. Although so little is known in regard to the Anonymous plan, there seems to be sufficient evidence to negative the idea propounded by Vertue that it was the work of Aggas. This idea he gained because a view of Oxford, drawn by Aggas in 1578, and published in 1588, speaks of his having had a desire to publish a plan of London, but (in 30 Queen Elizabeth, 1588) "meantime the measure, form, and sight I bring of ancient Oxford." A trained surveyor like Aggas would hardly have brought out an enlarged copy of Braun's map twenty years after the original. It is probable indeed, considering the spelling of the names, that Bagford's observation on the Anonymous plan, that it seemed to have been "done in Holland," is true. Mr. Thomas Dodd, in a MS. letter in the Crace Collection, points out a passage in Hakluyt where it is advised that the Pit and Jackman Expedition of 1580 should take with them the map of England and the "large Mappe of London." Mr. Dodd goes on to point out that Hakluyt also refers to Clement Adams as an engraver on wood, and he might have been the author of such a large map, which may be the Anonymous woodcut plan. Mr. Overall, in his inconclusive preface to the reproduction of the Anonymous plan, shows that Giles Godhed had submitted "the Carde of London," in 1562, to the Stationers' Company. We might conclude that this was a large plan on the same projection as Braun and Hogenburghe's plan, but this is uncertain, as just at this time there was published an engraved view of St. Paul's and the neighbourhood, of which there is a unique copy at the Society of Antiquaries. The most beautiful plan known to me, executed after the manner of Braun's cities, is a large plan of Bruges, signed by Marcus Gerard, pictor, 1562. Altogether I am inclined to think that there was such a plan of London existing before Braun's, and that the Anonymous plan is a coarse copy of one of those made in Holland for popular sale some time before 1580. Braun's plan, in any case, carries us back on firm ground to the end of the mediæval period, and by its aid we can check over our former results for an accurate plan of mediæval London.

Beyond this point we have an overwhelming mass of documentary evidence, by which the names of the streets, churches, and other landmarks, can be carried backwards by references in deeds, wills, patents, close-rolls, and Parliament-rolls, etc. etc. I have little doubt that almost every street and lane in London which existed in Stow's day could be carried back by this means to the thirteenth century, and a good many can be shown to have borne the same names in the century after the Conquest.

Then we have the complete list of city churches in the time of Edward I. given in the *Liber Custumarum*. The parish boundaries probably remain much as at that time, and the wards in their present form go back as far. It may be noted that a study of the boundaries shows that the parishes are in the main subdivisions of wards, and not that wards are aggregations of parishes. Such general documentary evidence can be further supplemented by the data which we have in regard to particular buildings which are still in part existing, or of which we have plans and other evidence.

We can accurately reinstate the City wall with its bastions and gates, the Bridge and the Tower of London. We have ample particulars as to the Cathedral and precinct of St. Paul's, with the line of the Close wall, the position of its gates, and the site of the Campanile in the north-east corner. The boundaries of the Conventual Establishments can be plotted, and the buildings within them can, in many cases, be laid down in detail. The plan of the Guildhall buildings may be reconstructed, and Hollar and Leeke's map gives the position of the Halls of the several Companies. An attempt has been made in the body of this work to sift out what can be learned of a still more remote London.

THE END

Footnotes:

[1] Mr. Green, from the long sections dealing with London in *The Making of England* and *The Conquest of England*, must be reckoned among the specialists on London. I shall often have to criticise Mr. Loftie's conclusions, but I do so merely because those are the views in possession at the present time. His books have the distinction of having revived an interest in London topography.

[2] *E.g.* Mr. Loftie's most recent book, *London Afternoons*.

[3] *Origines Celticæ.*

[4] Loftie, vol. i. ch. ii.

[5] Hearne actually says it is Long-town.

[6] Canon Isaac Taylor, *Dict. of Place-Names.*

[7] *Social England*, vol. i.

[8] Rhys, *Celtic Britain.*

[9] Ramsay, vol. i. p. 32.

[10] See Ludgate below.

[11] Now represented by Edgware Road.

[12] See *Dict. Nat. Biog.*, and De la Moyne Borderie.

[13] Thorpe's *Ancient Laws.*

[14] Joceline de Brakelonde, p. 56, cited by Wright.

[15] *Cal. St. Paul's MSS.*, Ninth Report Historic MSS. Com., p. 65.

[16] Rhys, *Celtic Britain*; Elton's *Origins.*

[17] Thomas Wright says the Billings, a Saxon people, settled at Billingsgate, and Mr. W. H. Stevenson derives the name from Billing, a Saxon name.

[18] There is probably some fact at the bottom of this story: perhaps the sword of St. Paul was carved on the Bishop's Gate. According to Geoffrey, the older Belinus had been placed in a golden urn on Billingsgate.

[19] Robert of Gloucester.

[20] See the story of Lludd in the Mabinogion.

[21] *English Hist. Rev.* vol. ii.

[22] *Episcopal Succession.*

[23] *Celtic Britain*, p. 124.

[24] C. F. Keary, *Vikings.*

[25] Asser.

[26] Asser.

[27] See Ramsay, *Foundations of England*, vol. i. p. 126.

[28] Compare Tame, Tamar, Teme, Tean, Teign. See *Surrey Collections*, vol. v.

[29] *Three Fifteenth Century Chronicles*, Camden Society.

[30] See Green, *Making of England*, vol. i. p. 105; *Surrey Collections*, vol. iii.; and *Athenæum*, 1901, No. 3838.

[31] *Polyolbion.*

[32] Bailey.

[33] *Calendar of St. Paul's MSS.*

[34] Dugdale's *Monasticon*, art. "Temple"; and Round's *Geoffrey de Mandeville.*

[35] *Transactions of London and Middlesex Archæological Society*, vol. iv.

[36] Hardy and Page, *London and Middlesex Fines*, vol. i. p. 3; see also Dugdale.

[37] *London and Middlesex Fines.*

[38] Kempe translates the same passage, "From the north angle of the City wall, where a rivulet of Springs near thereto flowing marks it out (*i.e.* the moor) from the wall as far as the running water which entereth the City" (*Sanctuary of St. Martin*).

[39] *Eng. Hist. Rev.*, 1896.

[40] A.S. dictionaries give *Wylle-burn* = Wellbrook.

[41] Other cases of churches called by personal names are St. Benet Fink, St. Martin Orgar, St. Martin Outwich, etc.

[42] St. Stephen's Walbrook is mentioned in a charter of *c.* 1100. See "Churches," below.

[43] Dr. Sharpe, *Letter Book A.*

[44] *Archæological Journal*, vol. i. p. 111.

[45] *Roman Antiquities on Site of Safe Deposit*, and *Roman Pavement in Bucklersbury*; see also *Archæological Review*, vol. iv.

[46] *Letter Book A.*

[47] Price, *Safe Deposit*, p. 30.

[48] *Origines Celticæ*, vol. ii.

[49] Sir J. H. Ramsay.

[50] Maitland sounded the river, and thought that there had been a ford at Chelsea; and the large number of Celtic and Roman

antiquities found from time to time at Battersea and Wandsworth incline me to the view that there was a passage here.

[51] Horsley's account of the Roman roads is still the best general authority; but see the *Antiquary* for 1901-2. The subject is being carefully re-examined in the new Victorian County Histories.

[52] Thorpe.

[53] The last, like all names compounded of "street," is a significant name wherever found.

[54] Clark, *Military Architecture*, vol. i. p. 31.

[55] Hardy and Page, *Fines*; and see Stow.

[56] *London and Middlesex Archæological Society Trans.*, vol. iii. p. 563.

[57] *London and Middlesex Fines.*

[58] Ackerman's *Westminster*, vol. i. p. 74.

[59] For Old Ford see *London and Middlesex Archæological Society Trans.*, vol. iii. p. 206.

[60] *Crawford Charters.*

[61] Bentley's *Cartulary of Westminster Abbey*, p. 4.

[62] See *Archæologia*, vol. xxvi., and, on the Tyburn, the *London and Middlesex Archæological Society Trans.*, vol. vi.

[63] *Surrey Collections*, vol. i.

[64] See Faulkner's *Chelsea*.

[65] Kemble, No. 872. See also Arnold's *Streatham*.

[66] *Eng. Hist. Rev.* 1898.

[67] See Rhys, *Celtic Britain*. The compiler of the pseudo-itinerary of R. of Cirencester writes Guethlin Street.

[68] It has been argued that if the Britons had chariots they must also have had roads; and it is generally held that the Icknield and other "Ridgeways" are of British origin. Mr. Boyd Dawkins has recently shown, from objects found in a camp with which the Pilgrim Way from Canterbury is associated, that this ridge-road is early Celtic at latest. It seems reasonable to suggest that it joined the Icknield Way, and that they formed an early road-system crossing the river at Wallingford.

[69] A paved way, thought to be the Watling Street, has just been found in Edgware Road. It was 20 feet wide, 3.6 below surface, and pitched with "boulders." A fragment was also found in Oxford Street.

[70] Kemble, *Codex Dip.* 591.

[71] Powell and Vigfusson's *Corpus.*

[72] I do not share this view as to Claudius and the bridge. Sir J. H. Ramsay even suggests that it may have been the work of Cunobeline.

[73] Roach Smith, *Archæological Journal*, vol. i. p. 112.

[74] Bruce, *Handbook to the Roman Wall.*

[75] See Price's *Bucklersbury.*

[76] *Making of England*, pp. 21, 105.

[77] Hermann, *De Mirac. S. Edmund*, p. 43; see *Eng. Hist. Rev.* vol. xii. p. 49.

[78] *Home Counties Mag.* vol. i.

[79] Leland.

[80] Earle, *Land Charters*; and *Codex Dip.* No. 280.

[81] *Cal.* p. 25.

[82] *Archæologia*, lii.

[83] In the A.S. dictionaries *Crepel* stands for an underground passage: there is said to be a Cripplegate on the Wansdyke.

[84] *Archæologia*, lii.

[85] Loftie's *London*, and *London* in "Historic Towns" series; maps in Green's *Short History*, and in Miss Norgate's *Angevin Kings*.

[86] It seems necessary to notice these points in such excellent books, as they are repeated in Sir W. Besant's *London*, p. 19, and more recent works, as if they were settled. Mr. Loftie, in a still later book, *London City* (1891), writes: "We know that Aldgate was opened about sixty years before FitzStephen's time. Aldersgate must have been made soon after the Conquest, and Cripplegate, with its covered way to the Barbican, cannot have been much later." In "Historic Towns" volume he says: "The foundations of the North Gate were lately found in Camomile Street. The massive masonry of the West Gate was also lately uncovered in Giltspur Street." In his *London Afternoons* Ludgate appears as probably the latest of the gates. All this is conjecture and, as I have shown, contrary to the evidence.

[87] *London and Middlesex Archæological Society Trans.* vol. iii.

[88] *Illustrations of Roman London.*

[89] Thorpe's *Ancient Laws.*

[90] Earle, *Land Charter.*

[91] W. de G. Birch, *London Charters.*

[92] Kemble, *Codex Dip.* No. 1074.

[93] Leland, *Coll.* vol. i.

[94] J. H. Round, *Calendar of French Documents.*

[95] J. H. Round, *Feudal England*, p. 320.

[96] *London and the Kingdom.*

[97] Pauli, *Pictures of Old London.*

[98] Price, *Hist. Guildhall.* In a deed, *temp.* Henry III., the Gildhall of the Cologne Merchants is said to be near Hay Wharf, for which see Stow.

[99] J. H. Round, *Calendar of French Documents.* See also *Soc de Waremanshaker* and St. Peter Ghent in Dugdale, vol. ii. p. 384.

[100] *Calendar of St. Paul's Documents.*

[101] Dugdale, vol. vi. p. 623.

[102] *Codex Dip.* ii. p. 3.

[103] *Heimskringla.*

[104] C. F. Keary, *Vikings*, p. 125.

[105] J. Earle, *Saxon Chronicles.*

[106] It is true it has been shown by Mr. Round that about two centuries later than this time *Arx* was a technical word for a military tower, and it is used by FitzStephen for the Tower of London itself: on the other hand, passages cited in *Domesday and Beyond*, p. 187, show that earlier it was convertible with *castrum* or *burh*, and it is beginning to be believed that *burh* means a *castrum* rather than a mound. Grants of property run, "within Burh and without Burh, on Street and off Street." Alfred himself writes of "Romeburh" and "Babylonburh."

[107] It is usually said that the members of the gild entered Holy Trinity Monastery, but this Mr. Round has shown is a misconception.

[108] Alfred Memorial volume.

[109] *Journal British Archæological Association*, 1900.

[110] *Domesday and Beyond*, p. 192.

[111] "I have been in White Hill in the Court of Cynvelyn" (Taliessin). According to a Triad it was Arthur who disinterred the head of Bran, disdaining to be so protected.

[112] Dr. Maitland, *Domesday and Beyond*.

[113] The Anglo-Saxon chronicler under 878 tells how Alfred made a *geweorc* at Athelney.

[114] As to the Danes holding the burh with London, see above, p. 68. I find London "and the Boro" mentioned together early in the thirteenth century.

[115] See G. R. Corner, *Archæologia*, vol. xxv.

[116] Saxon Chronicle.

[117] On the boundary of Paris Gardens was an embankment called the Old Broad Wall.

[118] See "House of Lewes Priory," *Archæologia*, vol. xxxviii.

[119] So well informed a guide as Baedeker says the Abbey was so named with reference to Eastminster by the Tower, which was only founded in the fourteenth century.

[120] See Sir J. H. Ramsay, vol. i. p. 422.

[121] See, for example, Hardy and Page, *London and Middlesex Fines*, p. 3. This volume also shows that Norton Folgate was formerly called Norton Folyot from a well-known family.

[122] *Calendar of St. Paul's Documents*, p. 25.

[123] A sixteenth-century London document has "stoop or post."

[124] *Athenæum*, 8th July 1899.

[125] Compare "portmeadows" and lands belonging to citizens elsewhere. At Colchester in 1086 there was a strip eight perches wide surrounding the town wall. As late as 1833 the borough of Bedford *included* "a broad belt of land." For a full account of the commonable fields of Cambridge and a discussion of the subject generally, see Maitland's *Township and Borough*. The London boundary was called the Line of Separation.

[126] The common pasturage of Westminster is mentioned in a charter.

[127] *London and Middlesex Archæological Society Trans.*, vol. v. See also for these documents Dr. Sharpe's *Letter Book C*.

[128] See also Stow's account of the alienation of common lands. Mile-End, according to Froissart, was "a fair plain place where the people of the city did sport them in summer."

[129] Fenchurch also seems to have been connected with this land, or at least the eastern suburb.

[130] The Friday fair of horses still lasted when Froissart wrote his account of Wat Tyler.

[131] *Township and Borough and Village Community.*

[132] Hudson Turner.

[133] *Making of England.*

[134] See Green's *Conquest of England.*

[135] In the summary of reigns at the end of Florence's Chronicle he speaks more than once of "London and the adjacent country" as going together.

[136] See L. Gomme, *Village Community*, p. 212.

[137] Munday. Loftie says there was another Romeland at Dowgate.

[138] *Calendar of Ancient Deeds.*

[139] See J. H. Round, *Commune of London*, p. 99.

[140] Riley, Sharpe, Loftie's two books, *French Chronicle of London*, notes.

[141] Or Langbourne and Fenny-about, as the east and west halves of this ward seem to have been sometimes called.

[142] Sharpe's *Calendar of Wills*, vol. i.

[143] *Calendar of Ancient Deeds*, vol. iii.

[144] *Riley's Memorials.*

[145] The *Liber Trinitatis* states that the precinct of Holy Trinity Aldgate was "of old" (pre-Conquest) one parish of Holy Rood. Two adjoining parishes are mentioned in a twelfth century charter (*Commune of Lond.* p. 253)—St. Laurence de Judaismo and St. Marie de Aldermanebury.

[146] *Judicia civitatis Londoniæ.*

[147] *Liber Albus*, p. 80.

[148] A document of about 1120-30 at St. Paul's gives us the name of "Salidus, Bedellus Warde."

[149] *Liber Albus*, p. 32.

[150] *Archæological Journal*, vol. iv. p. 278.

[151] Kemble, *Codex Dip.* 685.

[152] See Dugdale, who is wrong, however, in saying it was called a "Palatine tower." Stow applies this grant to Bridewell by mistake.

[153] See the genealogy as given by Mr. Round. It is interesting to find that the arms of Fitzwalter, the banner-bearer of London, a fess between two cheverons, is but a difference from the three cheverons of Clare.

[154] The arms of the Munfichets were similar to the arms of Clare, with the difference only of a label of five points. From this fact we may suppose that the families were allied. Munfichet Castle afterwards fell into the hands of the Fitzwalters.

[155] Howell's *Londinopolis*, 1657.

[156] Dr. H. J. Nicholson, *History of the Abbey of St. Albans*, Newcourt, and Maitland's *London*, vol. ii. p. 1051.

[157] Dr. Sharpe considers that the Royal was the name of a street near Dowgate, so called from La Reole, near Bordeaux.

[158] T. E. Price, *Safe Deposit*, p. 29.

[159] *Archæol.* xxix.

[160] J. Kempe, *Archæologia*, vol. xxiv.

[161] A large open Cheap is put in various parts by different writers. Mr. Joseph Jacobs, in an interesting inquiry as to the Jewry, makes the ground south of the Guildhall an open market.

[162] *Codex Dip.* i. p. 133. The Wilton Domesday gives a *Magnus Vicus* at Winchester.

[163] *Parentalia.*

[164] *London and Middlesex Transactions*, vol. ii.

[165] See J. E. Price, *Safe Deposit*. Price claims that the crypt found by Wren at Bow Church and described as Roman by him is not the now existing crypt. But the text and index of *Parentalia* plainly prove that the present church was built *on* it, and therefore it was the existing Norman structure.

Price says that remains of a bridge were found in Bucklersbury, and that a Roman road, possibly a continuation of that by Bow Church, passed here.

[166] Hudson Turner's *Domestic Archr.*, vol. i. App.; *Calendar of St. Paul's Documents*, Sharpe's *Calendar of Wills*, *Calendar of Ancient Deeds*, etc. In the last it is called Aphelingestrate in 1232.

[167] Dr. Sharpe's *Calendar of Wills*.

[168] Sharon Turner, *History of the Anglo-Saxons*.

[169] Alfred Memorial volume, 1899.

[170] Riley's *Memorials*.

[171] Issac.

[172] Godefroi's *Dictionary*.

[173] It is designed on the pattern of the famous monogram of Justinian, having for basis the letter N.

[174] Still more recent finds at St. Albans seem to show that here also the forum was an important building in the centre of the city.

[175] See account of Saxon Winchester in Hudson Turner's *Domestic Archr.*, vol. i., and of *Canterbury before the Conquest*, by Geoff. Faussett.

[176] Winton Domesday mentions Fishmongers' Street, Tanner Street, and Gold Street.

[177] *The Golden Legend.*

[178] Right through the Middle Ages the close of St. Paul's is called *Atrium S. Pauli*.

[179] *Parentalia.*

[180] Thorpes' *Analecta.*

[181] *Cotton Charters*, 11 Aug. 85.

[182] Richard of Cirencester, also Stow.

[183] See W. Maitland's *London*, and Green's *Conquest of England.*

[184] *London and Middlesex Archæological Society's Trans.* vol. ii.

[185] Sir H. Ellis, *Introduction to Domesday.*

[186] See *Eng. Hist. Rev.* vol. xvi.

[187] For the last see Round, *Geoffrey de Mandeville.*

[188] For many other churches mentioned in the twelfth century see *Calendar of St. Paul's Documents, Historical MSS. Reports*, which I have not drawn upon in this place. Several other churches may be presumed to be ancient from their dedication,

such as St. Pancras (destroyed at the great fire). Green (*Conquest of England*) attributes St. Augustine, St. Gregory, St. Benet, and St. Faith, to Bishop Erkenwald.

[189] For Strand churches see Sanders in *Archæologia*, vol. xxvi. Gibbs found work which he thought was Roman under St. Martin's-in-the-Fields. For an early foundation at Smithfield see Malcolm.

[190] Dugdale, under Bermondsey.

[191] The "Pedlar of Swaffham" and some Welsh stories refer to the bridge in the same way. See Rhys, *Celtic Folklore*.

[192] *Hist. MSS. Report of St. Paul's Documents*, p. 49.

[193] See T. H. Round, *Commune of London*.

[194] *Geoffrey de Mandeville*, p. 436.

[195] Thorpe, pp. 97-103.

[196] *London and the Kingdom.* In Winton Domesday is written *Chenictes tenebat la chenictehalla ubi potabant gildam suam.*

[197] Does this mean the lost charter constituting the mayor?

[198] *Camden Society.*

[199] Lick up the penny—Howell writes, "Some call London a Lickpenny, as Paris is called a Pick-purse, because of feastings and other occasions of expense."

[200] Book now disappeared. See for this and Stone generally, Price's *Roman Pavement in Bucklersbury*. It is not necessary that the note should be as old as the book.

[201] *London and Middlesex Archæological Society*, vol. v.

[202] *Parentalia.*

[203] This must be just the meaning of Berefridam—Burhfrid—Town-peace.

[204] *Domesday and Beyond*, p. 192.

[205] *Ibid.* p. 184.

[206] Lincoln also had a gerefa in the seventh century (Bede, ii. 6).

[207] *Geoffrey de Mandeville.*

[208] Maitland's *London* speaks of a list amongst the British Museum MSS.

[209] See Round in *Dict. Nat. Biog.* and *Commune of London.*

[210] F. Palgrave, *Rotuli Curiæ Regis*, vol. i. p. 12.

[211] Skeat says the weight was called from Troyes, but gives no conclusive reasons. See also *Notes and Queries*, 1871. Cripp's *English Plate* seems to prove this point.

[212] In Rolls Series.

[213] *Illus. Rom. Lond.* and valuable article, *Archæol.* xxix.

[214] There may have been a tower on the Bush Lane site: I am speaking of a large walled castrum.

[215] Like the one which has left us its bath in Essex Street, Strand. The 1681 Catalogue of objects in the Museum of the Royal Society describes a mosaic pavement found in Holborn near St. Andrew's.

[216] At Bucklersbury, described by Price.

[217] As many discoveries of walls and pavements have shown; as, for instance, at the south end of Bishopsgate Street, in Threadneedle Street, Lombard Street, at the Bank, the Royal

Exchange, Bucklersbury, Cannon Street, and the north side of Thames Street.

[218] Roach Smith in *London and Middlesex Archæological Trans.* vol i.

[219] I may say here that the drawing of the Roman pavement (Fig. 35) was originally made for Roach Smith by Fairholt.

[220] The mark P. LON. is first found on a coin of Diocletian.

[221] Other plans by A. Ryther, Norden, and Porter are small, and of little use except for giving the extent of suburban building at the moment of the execution of each.

www.ingramcontent.com/pod-product-compliance
Lightning Source LLC
Chambersburg PA
CBHW020154090426
42734CB00008B/818